TROUBLES AND TRIUMPHS
THE ROBERT YOUNG STORY

By Dan McGuire

Published in the USA by
BearManor Media
1317 Edgewater Dr. #110
Orlando, FL 32804
www.BearManorMedia.com

Softcover Edition
ISBN-10:
ISBN-13: 979-8-88771-076-1

Printed in the United States of America

For Joy, who brightens my darkest days.

CONTENTS

FOREWORD

I fell in love with movies back in the 1950s, when local television stations filled their schedules with dozens of black and white films, to match our black and white TVs; movies made in the 1930s and 1940s. One rainy summer afternoon I saw *The Maltese Falcon* for the first time. I have been a Humphrey Bogart fan ever since that day. In following his career, it baffled my adolescent mind how he would star in a major Hollywood film and often just costar in a typical Hollywood B picture.

Robert Young's career paralleled Bogart's in many ways. For example, in 1940 he was a costar in *Dr. Kildare's Crisis*, and in 1941 he was Ann Sothern's costar in *Maisie,* both B movies. But later that year he had a prominent role in the MGM super production of *Northwest Passage*, starring Spencer Tracy.

I was very aware of Robert Young's movie credits because of his hit television series *Father Knows Best*. It was truly a family program, and one my family watched every week to see how Jim Anderson, the father of the Anderson family, would navigate the problems, joys, and trials of what was considered an "average American family." I was about a year younger than Bud, the family son, so I had an electronic bond with the boy of the family. As portrayed by Robert Young, Mr. Anderson seemed to be in control of all the family's good, and not so good, times. He was the perfect father.

Robert Young's extensive movie career, as well as his very successful television series–add *Marcus Welby, M.D.* to his TV credits–made him a well-known personality. He was a talented and dedicated actor who was fortunate to have appeared in dozens of movies for several premier Hollywood studios. Unlike someone like Bogart, who has had many film festivals, tributes, and books dedicated to him, Robert Young has been nearly forgotten, and his chapter in the history of Hollywood is slowly fading away.

This book reinforces Young's place in the Hollywood history book, and that has been long overdue. It is virtually a celebration of the life and career of an actor, respected and well-liked by his directors and fellow thespians, who never won an Academy Award but didn't need one to be a success in a business where fame and glory are measures of greatness.

Bob Kolososki

Introduction: What's In a Name?

Soon after Henry Kissinger was appointed Secretary of State by President Nixon, he held his first press conference. A reporter asked, "Sir, how would you like us to address you?" Kissinger thought about it for a moment and replied, "'Your Eminence' has a nice ring to it."

A good name is generally deemed to be a valuable asset. Given that, us AARP-age folk tend to view the names being given to many of today's newborn as what the King of Siam called "a puzzlement." One wonders how these innocents will cope in their adult years with names as difficult to spell as to pronounce, much less to explain. Some may simply opt for a name change.

That's a common option in the entertainment world, where many singers, actors, and other performers take on names that bear little or no resemblance to those on their birth certificates. It was frequently the case in the heyday of the big Hollywood studios. Many wannabe actors and actresses assumed new or modified names, hoping to improve their chances of being "discovered." Others were signed by one of the studios and immediately rechristened with new monikers that were more appealing and more easily remembered.

Marion Robert Morrison sat tall in the saddle, but probably would not have become as popular a Western hero had he not become John Wayne. Likewise, a one-time shoe store clerk named Leonard Franklin Slye needed to rename himself Roy Rogers before becoming King of the Cowboys.

Lauren Bacall would have been less seductive with Humphrey Bogart as Betty Joan Perske. Emma Matzo's smoky voice was more suited to Lizabeth Scott. Gladys Marie Smith became "America's sweetheart" as Mary Pickford.

Archibald Alec Leach was more suave as Cary Grant. William Henry Pratt was more frightening as Boris Karloff. Laszlo Lowenstein was creepier as Peter Lorre. Emanuel Goldenberg was more menacing as Edward G. Robinson. Douglas Elton Thomas Ullman was more dashing as Douglas Fairbanks.

Some managed to reach stardom while holding on to their birth names, or something close to it. Ruth Elizabeth Davis became simply Betty Davis. Henry James Fonda just dropped his middle name and became one of Tinsel Town's most enduring stars. Brothers Wallace Fitzgerald Beery and Noah Nicholas Berry dropped their middle names and enjoyed successful screen careers. Wallace's MGM contract stipulated that he would always be paid one dollar more than their next highest paid star.

When MGM recruited Johnny Weissmuller to play Tarzan, producer Bernard Hyman said Johnny's name was "too long. We'll have to shorten it." His staff protested that Johnny was a world-famous Olympic swimming champion, and Hyman capitulated. "All right," he said, "then we'll just lengthen the marquee. And, put lots of swimming in the film!" Theaters did manage to get Johnny's name up in lights, and it undoubtedly drew many moviegoers who would otherwise have passed on a Tarzan flick. Each of Johnny's films included an exciting diving and swimming scene, whether it was fighting a threatening crocodile or a playful water ballet with a nude Jane (Maureen O'Sullivan).

When he signed his first contract with MGM, Robert George Young was doing live theater and had already shortened his name. Besides being an easy name to remember, Robert Young sounded like the name of an average guy-next-door, family man sort of fellow.

Because this book is about Robert, his name appears frequently. In an effort not to be too repetitive, I've sometimes used his full name, more often just Robert, or sometimes Bob. As early as his school years, he frequently used that name, and he was Bob to most of his fellow actors and other film coworkers. In numerous articles that I read about him, writers often started by giving his full name and then commenced referring to him by his last name: "Young starts his day…" Or: "Young says…" I've resorted to this a few times, but having grown up in an era when youngsters were admonished to address adults as "Mr. Smith" or "Mrs. Adams," I am a bit uncomfortable with it.

The name Robert Young seems just right for our subject. It served him well in over one hundred films and through a memorable career on radio and television…and it has a nice ring to it.

Dan McGuire

ROBERT YOUNG METRO-GOLDWYN-MAYER

THE YOUNG ROBERT YOUNG

On a wintry day in Chicago, the population of the Thomas Young family increased from five to six. Robert George Young was born on February 22, 1907.

His father, Thomas Edward Young, was a native of County Antrim in Ireland. As a young man, he emigrated to the United States. After passing through Ellis Island, he found his way to Chicago. There he met, romanced, and married a local girl, Margaret Cairn Fyfe.

Thomas was a building contractor. In the bustling growth of Chicago, it was a profession that provided steady work and a reasonably comfortable income. The Youngs purchased a roomy home in time to welcome their firstborn in 1889, a girl whom they named Marguerite Armour. Before Robert's grand entrance, his brother Thomas Allan was born in 1892 and brother Joseph Irving in 1900.

In between the arrival of the two brothers, their father traveled to Springfield, Illinois in May, 1898, and enlisted as a corporal in Company D of the 1st Illinois Calvary. He presumably expected to see action in the Spanish-American War, but that conflict was short-lived. He was discharged as a captain on October 11, 1898, and returned home to Chicago.

Although he was born there, Robert Young did not get to grow up and enjoy all the adventures of being a kid in that bustling city. While he was not quite one year old, his family left the city. It's not clear if there was a slump in his Chicago business, but Thomas Young elected to move his family to Seattle, Washington, another city that was experiencing growth.

It was there that the last of the Young children, Annette, was born in 1910.

By all reports, or lack of reports, the young Robert grew up a fairly normal, well-behaved lad. He was spared the disciplines of parochial school because his parents were Protestants, albeit seldom churchgoers. From age ten, he was sent to a Baptist Sunday school, but his only recollections of that were the rite of immersion, having a good attendance record, and learning to recite the Books of the Old Testament. Though he was never at the head of the class, there is no record of any difficulties or disciplinary action during his elementary school years.

In 1917, his father moved the family again, this time to Los Angeles, California. At ten years old, Robert made a smooth transition to a school there.

Family life underwent a more emotional and difficult transition that year. For reasons unknown, or never discussed by the family, Thomas Young simply left and abandoned them. He may have suffered from dementia or some mental illness. In November, 1927, he was admitted to what was then referred to as a "home." Discharged by year end, he was again admitted a year later. There is no record of precisely when he was released again, but it is known that for a time thereafter he lived in Santa Monica. He did not make any effort to reconnect with his wife and children.

Marguerite, Thomas and Joseph Young were of age to find various employments. They undoubtedly contributed toward the wellbeing of their mother. For his part, Robert was able to obtain a route delivering newspapers and turned over his modest income.

———

From as far back as his boyhood years, Robert Young remembered being an introvert. There may have been something in his genes. Or perhaps being the youngest of three brothers left him somewhat inhibited. Whatever the case, he was by nature a shy youngster, and it carried over into his teen years. But before he reached maturity, two wonderful things happened to temper that shyness.

After commencement from his grammar school, Robert became a student at Abraham Lincoln High School in Los Angeles. He took his studies seriously and was at least an average student in most classes, excelling in others. But although he made a few friends, he could not be described as especially outgoing. As a boy, he had become quite a bookworm, spending many hours at the local library. At Lincoln High, he spent much of his free period time in the school library, devouring both fiction and nonfiction. While it might not have been his conscious intention, it limited his interactivity with classmates.

Then he had the good fortune to sit beside an attractive red-haired coed named Elizabeth Louise Henderson in his 10th grade History class. In addition to being taken by his good looks, she detected in this quiet, self-contained classmate something that other girls may have been missing. Although quiet by nature, she was not as shy as Robert and was able to penetrate his reserved nature and strike up a friendship. It led to a relationship.

Years later, Bob would confess that his first impression of Betty was that she was "kinda dull" and "an awful bore." But she was not too dull to persist, and the two soon became a couple. Their youthful romance enabled Bob to open up a bit, and then Betty gave him a nudge that was destined to set a path for his remaining high school years and far beyond.

Abraham Lincoln High School, Los Angeles, as it looked in 1920s when Elizabeth Henderson and Robert Young were students; *Lincoln High School Alumni Association*

Betty was a member of a school activity called Playcrafters. As the name implies, it was an extracurricular group, sponsored and led by teachers, for students interested in producing and/or performing in plays. These were presented during school hours for students and repeated for parents at evening performances.

Aware of Bob's frequent escape into books, Betty suggested that he try reading some of the scripts that the Playcrafters had considered or actually performed. Then, with gentle but persistent encouragement, she persuaded her introverted boyfriend to join the group.

Hesitantly at first, but studiously, Robert began to participate in the production and practicing for the upcoming performance. To his surprise and great satisfaction, he soon discovered that he was putting himself wholeheartedly into this new activity.

As a newcomer, he was given a small role in his first performance, but the group's instructor saw something promising in this otherwise withdrawn young man. He was subsequently given larger parts with more spoken lines as the teacher sought to "bring him out of himself."

In the Playcrafters' 1926 presentation of *Taming of the Shrew*, Robert had the lead role of Petruchio, the tamer of Katherine. A yearbook report of the play says, "Bob Young gave his lines a zest that even Shakespeare, were he alive, would have commended."

The Playcrafters' presentation of *Sherwood* that same year was its largest production to date, with a cast of 125. Bob played Robin Hood and, in one of three acts, Betty got to be his Maid Marian. The yearbook critique says, "In an extremely difficult part to play, Bob Young did it so well that it is safe to say it was the finest piece of acting ever seen at Lincoln."

To his surprise, Bob found that he was able to completely submerge himself into whatever character he portrayed. He later professed that donning his costume and putting on makeup served as a shield for his shyness.

It may also have enabled him to participate in more student activities. In the 1926 yearbook of Abraham Lincoln High School, Robert Young is pictured on page 50. Next to his name and picture are accomplishments that include: "Head Yell Leader, Commissioner (Boys' Sports), Playcrafters, Lead in 'Taming of the Shrew,' 'Sherwood,' Leading Part in 'Briar Rose'." His classmates voted him the most likely to succeed in the theater.

The school's dramatics teacher had high praise for Robert's performances and urged him to pursue an acting career by enrolling in the School of Theatre Arts at the Pasadena Playhouse after graduation. Keenly aware of her beau's transformation on the stage, Betty encouraged him to listen to his teacher. This time he required little coaxing. Soon after he graduated from Lincoln High School, he registered for a four-year series of evening courses at the Playhouse.

In 1916, something called the Little Theatre Movement was causing small theater groups to spring up in towns and cities around the country. Actor-director Gilmor Brown gathered a troupe he named The Gilmore Brown Players and began producing a series of plays at a renovated burlesque theater. In 1917, he established the Community Playhouse Association of Pasadena, later to become the Pasadena Playhouse Association. Its creation necessitated a new venue for productions.

Community support was enthusiastic, and by 1924 the citizens of Pasadena had raised funds to build a new theater. It was located at 39 South El Molino Avenue. Designed in a Spanish Colonial Revival style by Pasadena artist and architect Elmer Grey, and completed in 1925, it boasted a fire curtain painted by Pasadena artist Alson S. Clark. It attracted national attention and boasted world premieres of works by Eugene O'Neill, William Saroyan, Noël Coward, F. Scott Fitzgerald and Tennessee Williams.

A School of Theatre Arts was established in the late 1920s and became an accredited college by 1937. During the school years, the Playhouse had as many as five independent stages in operation at any given time, giving more than 300 performances annually on the main stage alone. To provide housing for its many students, older homes along El Molino Avenue were modified to become dormitories.

The Pasadena Playhouse still functions as a community theater, presenting staged classic dramas, new musicals, and plays. Due to changes in Actors' Equity Association laws, and the opening of drama departments in many schools and universities across the country, the School of Theatre Arts shut down in 1969. But during its bustling years of operation it trained such notable future star alumni as Dana Andrews, Eve Arden, Raymond Burr, Don DeFore, Gene Hackman, Dustin Hoffman, Victor Mature, Joel McCrea, Leonard Nimoy, Lloyd Nolan, Tyrone Power, Randolph Scott, Robert Taylor…and Robert Young.

———

With a combination of enthusiasm and determination, Robert Young completed four years at Pasadena Playhouse. While training to be an actor might seem like fun and games to the uninitiated, it required as much study and effort as a more conventional college education. But performing arts college has many advantages for its students.

The school doesn't view performing arts as a mere extracurricular activity. The faculty are mostly working theater professionals with real-world experience. Instruction and lectures are sometimes given by visiting alumni who are established performers. Classes include such things as on-camera technique and preparing for auditions. Students get to showcase their talents in concerts, performances, exhibitions, and readings. Best of all, they are surrounded by like-minded artists who provide inspiration and encouragement of their creative pursuits. Many of these are likely to be colleagues and professional associates after graduation. Robert got to know a number of future actors, actresses and other film workers that he later would work with or see on studio lots.

There was no scholarship or family nest egg to pay for Robert's tenure at the School of Theatre Arts. To cover his costs, he worked at numerous part-time jobs throughout his four years. He was at times a drugstore clerk, a haberdashery salesman, a bank clerk, and a reporter. One wonders how he managed to be hired for the latter position, or how the mild-mannered Robert Young could have been a loan company collector. Perhaps he was applying his actor's training to perform in positions he otherwise would have found daunting.

During his schooling at the Pasadena Playhouse, he filled both minor and major roles in more than thirty stage productions. Most were by authors whose names are no longer familiar to playgoers. But Robert also appeared in works by Eugene O'Neill (*Lazarus Laughed* and *Marco Millions*), George Bernard Shaw (*Man and Superman*), Henrick Ibsen (*An Enemy of the People*), and Booth Tarkington (*The Plotocrat*).

After graduation, he joined a touring production company to earn a modest income while further honing his acting skills. Meanwhile, he listed himself as a freelance actor with various film studios and was gratified to be hired for a number of "extra" roles. Sharp-eyed audiences may even spot him in a couple of Keystone Kops comedies.

Extras in films are like sound effects on radio dramas. They appear as waiters, store clerks and shoppers, people strolling down a street, a face in the crowd, all nameless folk there to fill in background in various scenes. The pay is nominal, but parts require no lengthy rehearsals and usually just one day's work.

In 1928, Robert landed an extra role in Cecil B. DeMille's last silent film, *The Godless Girl*. It involved a teenage gang leader who gets sent to reform school. Robert received no mention in the film's credits, but as one of the gang members he appeared in several scenes.

Director Alfred Hitchcock was noted for making a brief appearance somewhere in the background of one minor scene in each of his films. He would be boarding a bus, walking through a hotel lobby, or stepping out of an elevator, often unnoticed by moviegoers who were not alert and looking for him. Years later, Robert quipped that in his first minor film role he had more on-screen time than Hitchcock did in any of his.

In 1931, still persevering as a regular with the touring stock company, Robert was performing in a now forgotten play called *The Ship*. A Metro-Goldwyn-Mayer talent scout was in the audience. He was impressed with Young's performance, liked his looks, and caught up with him after the show to arrange for a get-together.

They met for lunch, Robert gave the scout a summary of his experience, and they arranged for him to have a screen test. It turned out to be somewhat less than what the scout had led Robert to expect. He played what clearly was a minor role in a scene with a young actress who was auditioning for an actual film. Nevertheless, the brief session went well.

Then Bob was obliged to endure the anticipatory wait for a call from the studio. When it came, he met with several MGM executives who expressed their satisfaction with the "test" and made him an offer. It was an appealing offer. Robert left the studio lot with a smile on his face and a five-year contract in hand.

———

METRO-GOLDWYN-MAYER MEMORIES

As enthused as he must have been to become a contract performer for the prestigious Metro-Goldwyn-Mayer enterprise, Robert Young's timing was also auspicious. Filmmakers were in the early stages of mastering the technique for adding sound. Some films were being produced in two formats, one with sound and the other silent, to accommodate the many theaters that had not yet been equipped for sound. But "talkies" were the new thing.

Before he had time to learn his way around the MGM lot, Robert was loaned out to the Fox Film Company (later to merge with 20th Century Pictures as 20th Century-Fox). It was common practice for the studios to loan lower-tier actors back and forth when they had no current in-house assignment. Such on-loan arrangements were useful when studios had no suitable player available on their own lot to fill a supporting role. Moreover, there was a monetary incentive, since a negotiated dollar exchange was involved. Even while films were silent, money talked.

While being shopped out may have been disconcerting, Robert's first film as an MGM regular got him a free trip to Hawaii. Filmed in Honolulu, 1931's *The Black Camel* was based upon one of the many Charlie Chan mystery novels by Earl Derr Biggers. It starred Sally Eilers, Bela Lugosi, Dorothy Revier, and Warner Oland as Honolulu Police Inspector Charlie Chan. It was the first of sixteen films in which Oland starred as Chan. A reviewer years later wrote that the Chan pictures pretty much kept Fox afloat during the 1930s.

Robert Young plays Jimmy Bradshaw, publicity director for movie star Shelah Fayne, who is filming on location in Honolulu. He gets to outlive her, as she is murdered midway through the film. For the first time, the name Robert Young appears in the film's credits, albeit under those of the stars and in smaller letters.

Robert's next film, *The Sin of Madelon Claudet,* boasted a screenplay by Ben Hecht and the renowned Helen Hayes as its star. Robert plays a doctor whose neglect of his wife leads her to leave him. His friend Dr. Dulac is played by Jean Hersholt, who went on to fame as the star of radio's long-running series *Doctor Christian*. The cast also includes Lewis Stone, best remembered for his role as Judge James Hardy in the *Andy Hardy* film series.

In spite of his relatively minor role, Young probably was noticed by more moviegoers than would otherwise have filled the theaters thanks to the praise that was heaped upon Helen Hayes. She won an Academy Award for her performance as a wrongly imprisoned woman who turns to theft and prostitution in order to support her son.

Regarding his role, Robert later mused, "I really owe my first big opportunity to Irving Thalberg's technique of remaking pictures to his satisfaction. I was hired for a bit part as Helen Hayes' son in *The Sins of Madelon Claudet* and, after shooting was completed, Thalberg kept adding scenes and reshooting so that, by accident, my bit part became a significant role."

In light of the scenes and language that moviegoers accept as the norm today, it might seem strange that the plot of *Madelon Claudet* was considered rather risqué. But the film came out not long after the introduction of the Motion Picture Production Code, a set of industry guidelines for the self-censorship of content. Administered by Will H. Hays, who at the time was president of the Motion Picture Producers and Distributors of America, it became known as the Hays Code.

Hays, however, took a rather permissive attitude toward enforcement of the code. In 1934, faced with a public campaign condemning immorality in film content and the prospect of a government takeover of film censorship, the studios were forced to commit to greater oversight, and the Production Code Administration was created, headed by Joseph Breen. Thereafter, the content of film was more closely screened and the code more rigidly enforced.

That didn't prevent the selection of a title for Robert Young's next film. *Hell Divers* starred Clark Gable (sans moustache) and Wallace Beery as a pair of competing chief petty officers in early naval aviation. It mostly focused on exciting aerial sequences and was well received by audiences and reviewers alike. A *New York Times* reviewer effused over the "magnificently photographed production, one that includes naval air stunts and impressive landing feats." For aircraft enthusiasts, the film is considered an aviation classic. Robert Young appears as a pilot in a minor role near the end of the film.

In *The Guilty Generation*, Boris Karloff and Leo Carrillo star as competing New York bootleggers Tony Ricca and Mike Palermo. Tony's son Marco (Robert Young) and Mike's daughter Maria (Constance Cummings) fall in love, and a blood feud ensues. The plot only vaguely resembles *Romeo and Juliet*, but the bodies do pile up.

Leo Carrillo is best remembered for playing Pancho in the popular television series *The Cisco Kid*, which ran for 156 episodes from 1950 to 1956. He already was sixty-eight years old in 1949 when he first teamed with Duncan Renaldo to costar in five Cisco Kid movies.

The Guilty Generation probably was the least notable of Robert's first four films, but his role gave him more screen time than any of the others.

One highlight of the year might also have been meant by MGM as an opportunity to give Young some exposure to the Hollywood crowd and moviegoers. He was delegated to escort the beautiful actress Anita Page to a party at the Hollywood Roosevelt Hotel on August 4 to celebrate her twenty-first birthday.

Page was one of filmdom's most popular leading ladies during the last years of the silent screen era, having costarred with the likes of John Gilbert, Clark Gable, and Robert Montgomery. She starred in *The Broadway Melody* (1929), the first sound film to win the Academy Award for Best Picture. At the peak of her silent film stardom, she received more mail than any other female star except Greta Garbo. Yet she felt that "talkies" lacked the allure of the silents and retired after her next couple of films.

As frequently happens in Hollywood, Robert Young accompanying Page to such a special occasion set a rumor flowing as to a possible romance. It was short-lived, however. After all, Page was an adored star, and Young was, well, just a new young actor in town.

For office workers, store clerks, union laborers and others who are not self-employed, the end of the first year on the job usually brings a sense of accomplishment and relief that their satisfactory performance has earned them the opportunity to begin another year. Robert Young experienced these feelings upon completing his first year as a Metro-Goldwyn-Mayer regular. But mingled with his upbeat feelings was a sense of insecurity that was to haunt him throughout his years with the studio.

In part, that was just Young's innate shyness dampening his spirits. But being under the thumb of the studio bosses put pressure on all but the top stars. Even highly rated directors were at times considered replaceable. Actors and actresses who were "big box office," could negotiate special privileges along with handsome salaries. More lowly performers and film crews were ruled with an iron fist.

Robert was obliged to be available at all times. If he was to refuse a role for which he was chosen, he could be put on suspension. Actors who were suspended were prohibited from taking on any other employment to supplement their income, even something part-time that in no way was related to film-making. Young had no intention of refusing any reasonable role, but the oppressive working conditions of studio contract players made him uncomfortable–precisely the effect studio brass wanted to impose upon their underlings.

For Robert, 1932 started off with the role of a U.S. Treasury agent in *The Wet Parade*, based upon an Upton Sinclair novel. Once again he worked with Lewis Stone, and with stars Myrna Loy and Walter Huston. Jimmy Durante plays Young's quirky partner. The evils of alcohol become evident as we see its devastating effects on two families.

Ben Alexander, best remembered for his role as Officer Frank Smith in the *Dragnet* television series, has a supporting role. In 1952, Jack Webb, actor-producer-director of *Dragnet*, needed a replacement for Barton Yarborough, who had played Detective Romero opposite Webb's Sgt. Joe Friday. A few actors filled in as Friday's partners until Alexander appeared as Officer Frank Smith, first in the radio series, then in a film version and on television until 1959.

Although he played an upstanding government agent in *The Wet Parade,* the film proved to be prophetic for Robert Young. His consumption of alcohol would later become a long-running problem.

Because the Motion Picture Production Code was so loosely enforced until 1934, earlier films are often referred to as "pre-Code." That is the case for 1932's *New Morals for Old*, in which Robert Young appears with Myrna Loy and Jean Hersholt. Affluent New York City parents are distressed with their adult children's late hours and wild parties. The daughter takes up an affair with a married man and the son (Young) goes to Paris to be an artist. A brief scene that includes nudity, albeit in shadow, was considered bold at the time. Fast forward to the 21st Century.

Another pre-Code film that later might not have passed muster, *Unashamed* was based upon an actual Philadelphia society murder that was deemed an "honor killing." The film stars Helen Twelvetrees, Lewis Stone and Jean Hersholt. Twelvetrees was a stage actress who, like many others, came to Hollywood to replace silent screen stars who could not make the transition to talkies or simply chose not to. She plays a debutante whose brother (Robert Young) stands trial for killing her no-good lover.

Strange Interlude, based on a much longer 1928 play by Eugene O'Neill, starred Norma Shearer and Clark Gable. A romance between Nina (Shearer) and Gordon (Robert Young) is squelched by her stern father. When Gordon is killed in the war, she honors his memory by becoming a nurse in a veteran's hospital. Borrowing a technique used by Alfred Hitchcock in *Murder* (1930), the film voices a lot of the characters' inner thoughts. Done less smoothly, the actors' facial expressions and awkward pauses make the effort more comical than dramatic. It did not hold audiences spellbound. (But that proved to be a good title for a later film.)

The Kid from Spain is a musical comedy starring Eddie Cantor (sometimes in blackface, in an era when that was considered acceptable), Noah Beery, Sr., and J. Carrol Naish. Naish appeared in over 200 films, sometimes in starring roles, but he probably is best remembered for playing Luigi Basco on the popular radio program *Life With Luigi*. It was a light-hearted comedy about the mishaps of newcomer Luigi adapting to life in America. The program aired from 1948 to 1953, but eventually succumbed to complaints of Italians who failed to appreciate its gentle humor.

In *The Kid from Spain*, Eddie Cantor is somehow mixed up in a bank robbery and eludes the police with the help of his Mexican friend Ricardo (Robert Young). They flee to Mexico, where Ricardo passes Eddie off as a bullfighter. No surprise that the result involves a lot of comic bull.

Perhaps most noteworthy about the film are its musical scenes, directed and choreographed by Busby Berkeley, and an appearance by the Goldwyn Girls. Included in the group of lovelies are future stars Betty Grable, Paulette Goddard, and Jane Wyman, all uncredited.

Still treading softly because of his uncertainty about his status at Metro-Goldwyn-Mayer, Robert Young found some comfort in one small milestone. Although his roles were still minor, he had appeared in five films in 1932, one more than in 1931. He would surpass that in 1933.

His first film that year was *Men Must Fight*, starring Diana Wynyard, Lewis Stone and Phillips Holmes. After her lover is killed in World War I, a woman raises their son as a pacifist. However, when a second world war looms, that belief is put to the test. Robert Young plays Lt. Geoffrey Aiken. A Mrs. Chase is played by Hollywood gossip columnist Hedda Hopper in a cameo appearance.

Today We Live was a romance-drama film, loosely based upon a William Faulkner story and directed by Howard Hawks. It starred Joan Crawford, Gary Cooper, Franchot Tone and Robert Young, and marked the first time that Young received major credit, albeit not top billing. While on shore during World War I, two Naval officers compete for the same beautiful young woman. Then their submarine is sent with the rest of the flotilla to fight in the Adriatic Sea.

Irving Thalberg, then vice-president of MGM, had Crawford written into the script because her contract cost the studio $500,000 whether she worked or not. Crawford, in turn, insisted upon Cooper as her costar at a time when he was in a bit of a decline. Crawford met her future husband, Franchot Tone, on the set of the film and they married two years later.

Hell Below (there's that word again) is another World War I drama about submarine warfare. It starred Robert Montgomery, Walter Huston, Madge Evans and Robert Young, once again with a bit more noticeable role. In between action scenes, lower ranking officers are obliged to attend a ball and dance with the wives of admirals. It affords some humor and a bit of romance involving one admiral's daughter. Jimmy Durante is on board to add some lighter moments as the Ships Cook, nicknamed "Ptomaine."

Tugboat Annie starred Marie Dressler, Wallace Beery, Robert Young and Maureen O'Sullivan. Dressler and Beery were MGM's most popular screen team at the time, having starred together in 1930's bittersweet *Min and Bill*. For her role in that film, Dressler won the Academy Award for Best Actress. In this film, the duo are a comically quarrelsome middle-aged couple who operate a tugboat. Robert Young and Maureen O'Sullivan are the requisite pair of young lovers that tugboat captain Annie tries to help get it together.

Loaned out to Universal Pictures, Robert rated top billing for his role as a Western University football hero in *Saturday's Millions*. Johnny Mack Brown (one-time star in the Alabama backfield) and several other real players lend reality to some exciting gridiron scenes. Andy Devine provides some comic relief. Robert's winning heroics are performed by a stunt double. Both Alan Ladd and Walter Brennan appear in small uncredited roles.

Once more shopped out to another studio, Robert finished the year starring in *The Right to Romance*, an RKO Radio Pictures release. His costar, Ann Harding, was a popular Broadway and regional theater actress in the 1920s, and one of the first actresses to gain fame in the new medium of "talking pictures." She was nominated for the Academy Award for Best Actress in 1931 for her work in the film *Holiday*.

The Right to Romance is one of several "lost RKO films" that were unearthed and re-released in 2007 by Turner Classic Movies. Along with *Tugboat Annie*, it is notable as one of the rare films in which Robert scores a romantic triumph in his early years. In action films, his roles tended to be secondary characters who were buddies of the hero, and subject to various dramatic death scenes. In romance films, he was apt to compete (unsuccessfully) with another male lead, or he might be a best buddy who helps his pal win over the female lead. Commenting upon this aspect of Young's screen image, Louis B. Mayer once remarked, "He has no sex appeal." Mayer observed that in films that involved a romantic competition, Young came across as the type of guy who never got the girl.

While still a nervous newcomer, Robert once had a rare opportunity for a one-on-one chat with the great man. Mayer said, "Bob, I've been thinking about you and watching your work. A couple of things I think that you should do, for your career and for us." Always wanting to improve, and eager to learn, Robert sat on the edge of his chair as Mayor continued, "Put on a little weight and get more sex."

Mayer went on to suggest that Bob rent an apartment in Hollywood, host some wild parties and be seen around town dating and dining with a lot of beautiful young women. He said MGM had dozens of lovely wannabe starlets who would be pleased to step out with him.

It wasn't the sort of advice that Robert had been hoping for or anticipated. He had been trying to put on weight since high school, but his body seemed to have decided that he was in no need of bulking up. He was still living at home with his mother. While he probably could afford a Hollywood apartment, wild parties did not appeal to him.

As for dating a lot of hopeful young actresses, that was not going to fly with Betty. When he hesitantly related to her his conversation with the big boss, her response was, "Fine. When this has all blown over, if it ever does, give me a ring sometime."

Robert chose to continue living with Mom, and decided that he would have to further his career by broadening and perfecting his acting skills.

———

Like beauty, however, sex appeal is in the eye of the beholder. Throughout Bob's years at the Pasadena Playhouse, touring and working "extra" parts in silent films, he and Betty were a steady couple and together as much as possible. Sometime in 1932, emboldened by his MGM contract in spite of his persistent insecurities, Bob asked Betty to marry him. It's not known if Betty replied, "I thought you'd never ask." Nevertheless, she accepted.

On March 6, 1933, in Orange County, California, Elizabeth Louise Henderson, formerly of Evansville, Indiana, became Mrs. Robert Young. It was an informal event, performed by a justice of the peace in Santa Ana. Given Robert's status in the MGM empire at the time, the event did not make national headlines, although it may have rated a mention in Hedda Hopper's Hollywood gossip column.

In anticipation that their union would result in one or more additions to the household, Bob and Betty purchased a large home (6,000 square feet) in Beverly Hills. In addition to four bedrooms and five baths, it boasted a large den (what today would be called a family room) in which Bob installed a movie projector and screen.

Robert began another productive year in 1934 with his role as Will Connelly in Fox Film's *Carolina*, with Lionel Barrymore and Joanna Tate. During the Reconstruction period after the Civil War, the Connelly family regains some of it former status when Will marries a Yankee farm girl (Tate) over the objections of his father (Barrymore). This being what is referred to a B picture, Young was allowed to get the girl.

Stepin Fetchit appears in one of the semi-comic roles that Black actors often were obliged to accept if they wanted to work in films. Appearing unaccredited are a very young Shirley Temple as Joan Connelly and a fellow named Roger Moore, playing an army officer. More about him later.

In the RKO Pictures film *Spitfire*, Ralph Bellamy and Robert Young are engineers heading up the construction of a dam in the mountains. They both are attracted to a local hillbilly "spitfire" named Trigger Hicks (Katherine Hepburn) who is a faith healer. Things get tense when the town folk begin to suspect that she is actually a witch.

The House of Rothschild was a 20th Century Pictures film that chronicled the rise of the Rothschild family of European bankers. It starred George Arliss, Loretta Young, Boris Karloff, and Robert Young. This was one of Hollywood's "message" films, an account of how the wealthy Rothschild family endures prejudice from the anti-Semitic society in which they live. That subject was dealt with more directly in 1947's *Gentlemen's Agreement*, starring Gregory Peck.

Back on the MGM lot, Robert joined Ted Healy and Nat Pendleton in *Lazy River* as a trio of escaped convicts who find their way to a Cajun village. There they meet Sarah Lescalle (Jean Parker), sister of another convict, who is trying to keep his little shrimping business afloat. A local bad guy plots to take over her dock, but the boys succeed in setting him adrift.

In MGM's *Hollywood Party*, Robert is about the only one playing it straight. The film is a musical comedy with Jimmy

Durante playing "Schnarzan," a parody of Tarzan, who needs to replace his aging lions. A wild party involves many guests, including a "lion provider." The film involves a series of segments that include nonsense by Laurel and Hardy, the Three Stooges, and Mickey Mouse (voiced by Walt Disney). Robert keeps his cool, playing it straight as a radio announcer.

Loaned out to Columbia Pictures, Robert Young joined Walter Connolly and Doris Kenyon as siblings John, Jack and Margaret Forrester in *Whom the Gods Destroy*. An ocean liner sinks, and a famous theatrical impresario acts heroically, saving many lives, before panicking and dressing as a woman to escape. Upon his safe return home, he must deal with his act of cowardice. Walter Brennan appears in a brief uncredited role.

Back again at MGM, Robert shared top billing in *Paris Interlude* with Madge Evans, Otto Kruger, Una Merkel, Ted Healy and Louise Henry. Perhaps the most notable thing about the picture is the number of stars in a rather forgettable tale. Julie (Evans) has a star-crossed romance with Sam (Kruger). When he is believed dead, her friend Cassie (Merkel) urges her to take up with good guy Pat (Young). Then Sam reappears.

Still on the MGM lot, Robert starred as ace baseball player Larry Kelly in *Death on the Diamond*. Pop Clark (David Landau) will lose his team, the St. Louis Cardinals, unless they win the pennant and he can pay off a debt to mobsters. Recognizable to many baseball fans, but unaccredited, are a number of former Cardinals and Chicago Cubs players. Also unaccredited, Walter Brennan as a hot dog vendor, Roger Moore as Cardinals player #11, and Dennis O'Keefe as a radio announcer.

It's three in a row now for Robert as he stars with Stuart Erwin, Leo Carrillo, Betty Furness, Ted Healy and Preston Foster in another MGM film, *The Band Plays On*. Four boyhood buddies, junior classmen at Pacific University, are star players on the school's football team and dubbed The Four Bombers.

Stuart Erwin had been active in silent films as early as 1928. In 1932, he co-starred with Bing Crosby in the comedy *The Big Broadcast*. He was nominated for Best Supporting Actor in the 1940 Academy Awards for his portrayal of a dairy delivery man in the film adaptation of Thornton Wilder's play *Our Town*. Yet he probably is best remembered for his many radio appearances and 1950's short-lived television series *The Stu Erwin Show*, in which he costarred with his real life wife, June Collyer.

MGM may have been seeking an avant-garde appeal with the lower-case spelling of its *La ciudad de cartón*. A frustrating search turned up little information on the film except that the title is loosely translated *The Cardboard City* (presumably referring to Hollywood) and it starred Janet Gaynor, Lionel Barrymore, and Robert Young, as themselves.

It had been a busy year for Robert. On their own lot or elsewhere, MGM had kept him productive working on ten films. Although they all fell into the B picture category, he had starred or shared top billing in most of them.

It also had been a productive year on the home front, as Bob and Betty welcomed the arrival of daughter Carol Anne. Now another of those four bedrooms would be occupied.

In his first film of 1935, MGM's *West Point of the Air,* Robert Young shared top billing with several well-known stars: Wallace Beery, Lewis Stone, Maureen O'Sullivan, Rosalind Russell, and Robert Taylor. In a drama about U.S. Army Air Corps pilot training, a gruff Army sergeant inspires his son (Young) to become an ace flyer. Walter Brennan makes another unaccredited appearance as a soldier. Younger readers are more likely to remember Brennan as Grandpa Amos in the 1957-1963 television series *The Real McCoys.*

Robert next starred with Evelyn Venable in MGM's romantic comedy *Vagabond Lady.* Josephine Spiggins (Venable) works in a department store and is considering marriage to the stuffed-shirt son of the owner. Then his free-spirit brother returns from sailing the South Seas in his boat, Vagabond Lady. *Photoplay* magazine commented that Robert had "a kind of sparkle that he must continuously repress before the cameras when playing a serious role."

Calm Yourself (MGM) is a comedy film starring Robert Young, Madge Evans, Betty Furness, Ralph Morgan, and Nat Pendleton. Preston Patton's favorite piece of advice is "Calm yourself." Fired from his advertising job, Patton (Young) has a bright idea to start a business helping harried customers relax. As might be expected, his efforts go comically awry and his clients become even more stressed. Betty Furness has a supporting role, and Ward Bond makes an uncredited appearance as a detective.

A versatile actress of screen, radio and television, Betty Furness is perhaps best remembered for a mishap on television's *Studio One* series. She was the spokeswoman who did commercials for sponsor Westinghouse. One live spot featured a refrigerator door that refused to open, causing one of the most infamous bloopers in TV history. It wasn't her fault, but Betty was teased about it for years, until 1981, when she set the record straight, noting that she had been off that day and look-alike actress June Graham had filled in for her.

Barbara Stanwyck is the predominant star of MGM's comedy *Red Salute.* She plays the rebellious daughter of a U.S. Army general who becomes involved with a suspected communist agitator. Out of cash and stranded in Juarez after a wild weekend, she is picked up by a soldier (Robert Young) who escorts her home. They are, initially, at odds. He says she deserves to be shot. But, of course, love has a way. They honeymoon in his trailer.

In the Universal Pictures film *Remember Last Night?*, Robert Young shared billing with Edward Arnold and Constance Cummings. The venerable British actor Arthur Treacher appears in one of his many roles as a butler. After a wild party, a group of friends awaken to find their host murdered. When the police arrive, they are unable to remember much about the night before.

Because the recently activated Production Code restricted the drinking of alcohol onscreen, some scenes had to be modified or scrapped, and even the word "hangover" was expunged from the dialogue. The toned-down scripting may have contributed to the film's mixed reviews and poor box office results.

The Code had gone into effect just weeks after the release of the classic film *The Thin Man.* Had that film been similarly restricted, William Powell and Myrna Loy would have been hard-pressed finding something to do with their hands in many scenes.

Meandering from the Universal lot over to Paramount Pictures, Robert joined stars Claudette Colbert and Fred MacMurray in the romantic comedy *The Bride Comes Home.* After her father's business goes bankrupt, Jeannette Desmereau (Colbert) is hired by two young men as a front in their plan to start a magazine. Love ensues, but it is three-sided. The film got mostly good reviews, but Robert and Fred received less praise than the lovely Claudette. One reviewer said, "Miss Colbert is the most charming light-comedy actress on the screen."

After his previous year appearing in ten films, Robert may have felt that he had been underutilized in 1935. That could only have added to the sense of insecurity that he quietly carried like a weight on his shoulders. Nevertheless, he was growing used to the routine of taking on whatever roles he was assigned, on his home lot at MGM or wherever he was loaned.

Meanwhile, for all his burdensome shyness, he was making friends with many of the stars and others with whom he worked. He was popular with both directors and other performers because of what they saw as an admirable work ethic. He was hard working and well prepared; he knew his lines and always hit his mark. Directors observed that he was game to appear in romantic roles, serious or costume dramas, screwball comedies, or three-hankie weepers. Fellow actors appreciated that he never attempted to steal a scene.

Whatever his secret misgivings, Robert Young was establishing himself as a dependable and appealing actor.

———

Robert Young began 1936 starring along with Betty Furness, Raymond Walburn, Thurston Hall, Bruce Cabot and Donald Meek in MGM's *The Three Wise Guys*, scripted by Damon Runyon. The son of a railroad tycoon is the target of a trio of con artists as he comes to the rescue of a pretty girl who faints on the train. The plot is as wacky and as convoluted as any of Runyon's short stories.

Next, Bob was not only loaned out, but shipped out, to England. Alfred Hitchcock had made a specific request to borrow him for his film *Secret Agent*. Bob and Betty decided to go together. They left Carol Anne in the care of a full-time nurse at home and headed for London, planning to see some of the sights together and perhaps some of the countryside.

Years later, Robert recounted to film critic Leonard Maltin that, upon their arrival, they were invited to meet Hitchcock at his studio office. Peter Lorre was there. He was to co-star with Robert. As they greeted one another, Hitchcock pressed a button on his desk and a man brought in a cart and served tea to everyone. The group chatted amiably for awhile, getting acquainted. When Hitchcock finished his tea, he scooted his chair over to the window and tossed out the cup and saucer.

Bob and Betty looked at one another with raised eyebrows. Then Lorre finished his tea, got up and walked to the window, and tossed out his cup and saucer. The Youngs concluded that it was some sort of British custom. For their part, they placed their empty cups on the edge of Hitchcock's desk. Bob told Maltin that he thought Hitchcock looked a bit disappointed.

Later that week, Hitchcock invited the Youngs to a small dinner party at his home. At the end of the meal, everyone retired to the large drawing room. As folks chatted, a butler came in with a humidor and offered cigars to the men. On his way out, as he passed Betty, she reached out and tapped his arm to stop him. Bob recalled that the poor man almost dropped the humidor.

Nervously, he looked to Hitchcock, who gave one of his Buddha-like nods.

Betty selected a cigar and remarked, by way of explanation, that back in the states many women in the South smoked pipes. A bit of an exaggeration, and it ignores the difference between pipe and cigar tobacco. Nevertheless, conversation diminished as she selected a cigar, sniffed it, and bit off the end. Then she put it in her mouth and nodded to the butler, who lit it for her and quickly withdrew.

She took an initial puff, blew out the smoke, looked pleased, and held up the cigar to admire it. Her audience was rapt as she nodded her approval to Bob, who struggled to keep a straight face. Betty took another leisurely puff, then another. She was able to carry it off for five or six puffs before taking in one too large and starting to cough. With a guilty grin, she passed the cigar to Bob, who snubbed it out in an ashtray as she confessed, "Well, I really don't smoke."

Until then, she had everyone hooked, including Hitchcock. He loved it, and afterward congratulated her on a superb performance.

The filming of *Secret Agent* went well. In addition to Peter Lorre, Robert had the good fortune to work with Madeleine Carroll and John Gielgud in the British International Pictures film. Three British agents are assigned to assassinate a German spy, but two of them become conflicted by doubts of conscience. Lilli Palmer has a minor role. Michael Redgrave makes an uncredited appearance, and Michael Rennie makes his film debut. The film is replete with Hitchcock themes, including mistaken identity, trains, and a "Hitchcock blonde."

But when filming was almost finished, someone brought word to Bob that he'd been loaned out for another film at the Gaumont-British Distributors studios. He was furious. Anticipating that he and Betty would be returning to their young daughter, he would now be in England for another six or eight weeks.

Back at their hotel, he was fuming. Betty let him rave for a bit, then said, "There isn't anything you can do about it. Why don't you just go ahead and do it and have a good time? I hear that Jessie Matthews [who would co-star] is very popular."

Robert took her advice and found that he was charmed by both Jessie and her husband Sonnie Hale. They had a delightful time working together, although filming ran weeks past the schedule.

In *It's Love Again*, Robert plays gossip columnist Peter Carlton. Faced with a deadline and a blank page, Carlton invents a socialite named Mrs. Smythe-Smythe whose hobby is big game hunting, jumping out of airplanes and driving men wild with her beauty. His jaw drops when aspiring actress Elaine Bradford (Matthews), in search of her big break, appears on the scene impersonating the incredible made-up lady. Britain's beloved Terry-Thomas, in an early uncredited role, appears as a dancer.

Reviewer Graham Greene effused that the "Oriental party" scene, filled with double entendre conversation, is worth the price of admission.

———

The majority of Alfred Hitchcock's actors and actresses had a minimalist approach that suited his formalistic style of filmmaking. It added a realism that evoked an emotional response from the audience. Hitchcock personally chose Robert Young to star in *Secret Agent*. While promoting the film to the press, he explained: "One of Hollywood's greatest failings is the way it allows its stars to get into a groove. When an actor achieves fame in some particular part, the tendency is to grind out all his future roles in the same pattern. When Robert Young came to England to work for me in *Secret Agent*, he had never appeared in a film as anything more than himself. In this picture I gave him a chance to give a genuine characterization, with the result that, in the final sequences of the picture, he developed a power and a conviction that would have done credit to Spencer Tracy."

Given the diversity of roles that Robert had filled until then, Hitchcock's evaluation of him is a bit condescending. True, Young did not have the masculine allure of Clark Gable, the suave charm of Cary Grant, the tough guy menace of James Cagney, or the swashbuckling bravado of Errol Flynn. He tended to come across as a Mr. Nice Guy. Yet he managed to adapt that persona to roles he played whether the film was a comedy, a romance, a mystery, or a buddy pic. Nonetheless, Hitchcock's satisfaction with Young's performance in *Secret Agent* was high praise. Soon after Hitchcock came to America, Bob and Betty had him to their home as a dinner guest.

———

Working with Alfred Hitchcock and meeting with his approval had to be gratifying, but it did not prevent Robert from working under a presumed cloud. In spite of the opportunity for he and Betty to see a bit of England, he was convinced that his being sent there meant that the MGM bosses were preparing to dump him.

It didn't happen. Back in Hollywood, he was sent to the RKO Pictures lot to costar with Barbara Stanwyck and Gene Raymond in *The Bride Walks Out.* In what appears to be a revamped version of 1931's *Ten Cents a Dance*, a former fashion model (Stanwyck) takes up a secret job when she realizes that her new husband cannot support her in the fashion to which she chooses to be accustomed. Ward Bond as a taxi driver and Dennis O'Keefe in a night club scene make uncredited appearances. Hattie McDaniel plays one of her many stereotyped roles, a maid.

In MGM's *Sworn Enemy*, Young stars as a law student who takes a job as a rich man's chauffeur. As luck would have it, his boss has a beautiful daughter (Florence Rice) and—wouldn't you know it?—love ensues. Dennis O'Keefe as a bandleader and Roger Moore as a reporter make uncredited appearances.

Without having to leave the MGM lot, Robert next starred in *The Longest Night* with Ted Healy, Julie Haydon, Catherine Doucet and Janet Beecher. The son of a department store owner falls for an attractive clerk. When burglars lock the pair in a storage room, she cleverly brings the fire department and cops to the rescue by setting off the fire alarm. This was MGM's shortest feature film, just fifty-one minutes, making its title a bit ironic.

On loan to 20th Century-Fox, Robert next starred with Shirley Temple in *Stowaway.* An orphan named Ching Ching (Temple) accidentally is stuck onboard when a ship leaves China headed for the United States. Wealthy playboy Tommy Randall (Young) finds her and assumes the role of her guardian, assisted by his valet, Atkins (Arthur Treacher). Alice Faye, star of dozens of musical films and wife of singer/bandleader Phil Harris, provides a love interest.

Sworn Enemy stars Robert Young and Florence Rice; *Stephen Cox* collection

En route, Shirley impersonates Ginger Rogers (with a life-sized Fred Astaire doll affixed to her toes), Eddie Cantor, and Al Jolson singing "Mammy." The curly-haired cutie was America's darling, and from 1934 to 1938 she was Hollywood's number one box office draw.

In later years, having retired from acting, Ms. Temple became politically active and was elected to Congress. She was appointed Ambassador to Ghana by President Gerald Ford, serving from 1974 to 1976. From 1989 to 1992, she served as Ambassador to Czechoslovakia under President George H. W. Bush.

Although Robert Young shared top billing with Temple in *Stowaway*, she really was the star. But he also shared a lot of on-screen time with her, and the picture was seen by more people than any other film in which he'd yet appeared. It couldn't hurt.

Robert renewed his contract with Metro-Goldwyn-Mayer in 1936, so whatever his concerns about his status, he had reasonable assurance of on-going employment. Yet his days were filled with worry that MGM might be on the verge of dumping him.

———

Back on the MGM lot, Robert Young began 1937 by joining Ann Sothern, Reginald Owen, Cora Witherspoon, and Dean Jagger in the romantic comedy *Dangerous Number*. While visiting Japan, Hank (Young), a clothing manufacturer, learns a formula for producing synthetic silk. Hank's wife Eleanor is played by Ann Sothern, later to become better known as "Maisie" (see more on that later). Eleanor has some friends who stir things up in their marriage. Disguised as a taxi driver, Hank drives the car into a lake and Eleanor's silk dress disintegrates! How did that get past the Code office?

Scene from *I Met Him in Paris*. From left, Robert Young, Claudette Colbert, Melvyn Douglas; *Stephen Cox collection.*

Claudette Colbert and Melvyn Douglas costarred with Robert Young in Paramount Pictures' romantic comedy *I Met Him in Paris*. Fashion designer Kay Denham (Colbert) saves up for a trip to Paris, where she meets playwright George Potter (Douglas) and playboy Gene Anders (Young), who compete for her affections. The film had the distinction of being the first screened at Washington, D.C.'s Newton Theatre when it opened in the Brookland neighborhood on July 29, 1937.

In MGM's romantic comedy *Married Before Breakfast*, inventor Tom Wakefield (Robert Young) has just sold a hair-removal formula for big bucks. Seeking to do good deeds for friends and strangers alike, he plots to speed up the marriage of Kitty Brent (Florence Rice) to her reluctant fiancée Kenneth (Hugh Marlowe). His efforts go comically awry. As he and Kitty realize that they have fallen in love, he tells her there's still time to get married today.

In *The Emperor's Candlesticks* (MGM), Robert joins Maureen O'Sullivan and William Powell in a story about spies from opposing sides who fall in love in pre-revolutionary Russia. A male Polish secret agent and a female Russian secret-police spy smuggle messages to St. Petersburg in candlesticks. While chasing after stolen candlesticks, they discover each other's identity and fall in love. But can love overcome their conflicting allegiances?

In the MGM comedy *The Bride Wore Red*, streetwise bargirl Anni (Joan Crawford) passes herself off as an aristocrat at a posh Alpine resort. Though she pines for the town postman (Franchot Tone), she plans to land a wealthy husband (Robert Young). From its love-vs.-security theme, to its knockout clothes, this is a quintessential woman's picture. It was the last of seven films that Crawford would make with her then-husband Franchot Tone.

In the dramatic film *Navy Blue and Gold* (MGM), Robert stars with James Stewart, Lionel Barrymore, Billie Burke, and Dennis Morgan. The plot revolves around the experiences of three young men attending the United States Naval Academy, where they learn the meaning of leadership, teamwork and competition, both on the gridiron and beyond.

With one exception, MGM was able to utilize Bob in half a dozen films without farming him out to another studio. That was somewhat soothing to his nagging sense of insecurity. He was able to work with and become better acquainted with more actors and film crews, and got to know and befriend others.

He was playing the lead or co-starring in the majority of his films, but most of these were in the B picture category referred to as "programmers." In an era when double features were the norm at most movie theaters, these were meant to be screened ahead of the A picture that was billed as the main feature. Robert's status as a second-tier star continued to be a worrisome issue for him.

Stars of *The Bride Wore Red*. From left, Robert Young, Joan Crawford, Franchot Tone; *Stephen Cox collection*

A Family Matter

Joseph Irving Young, Robert Young's older brother, was born September 21, 1900, in Chicago. By the time he had reached adulthood, the Young family had moved first to Seattle, Washington, and then to Los Angeles, where his father would later abandon them.

Even before his younger brother began his tentative acting career, Joseph appears to have been attracted to the stage. There is no record of what his full-time occupation was, but it evidently afforded him the time to enroll himself as an available "extra" with several film studios. Beginning as early as 1924, he began appearing in small parts in silent films.

Although the majority of his roles were uncredited, he initially worked under the name Joe Young. (This was long before the making of 1949's film *Mighty Joe Young*.) Between 1924 and the 1950s, he appeared in 243 films. His last role was as a chauffeur in 1953's *Gentlemen Prefer Blondes*.

In earlier years, he became a frequent victim of shenanigans in the comic films of Our Gang and the Three Stooges. (Did the studios pay a stipend to extras who got hit in the face with cream pies and had to send their suits to the cleaners?)

Occasionally he got a more noticeable part, as when he appeared aboard ship in 1935's *Mutiny Ahead*. While films were still silent in 1927, he played an actor in Mack Sennett's *The Girl from Everywhere*. Nipping at the hand that fed him, Sennett's wacky comedy was a spoof of filmmaking. The highlight of the film was a segment filmed in Technicolor that featured the famed Sennett bathing beauties. A very young Carole Lombard (with her first name spelled "Carolle") appeared in a part as small as Joe's. In 1940, he got to play a villain in Columbia Pictures' fifteen-chapter serialized thriller *The Shadow* (he of comic strip fame).

Sometime in the 1930s, the brothers Joseph and Robert Young had some sort of falling out. It was rumored at the time that Joseph's wife might have been involved. This seems unlikely, given Robert's long-running romance and subsequent marriage to Elizabeth Henderson. Moreover, Joseph broke off all relations with his entire family. He had his name legally changed to Roger Moore and worked under that name thereafter, although still uncredited more often than not. (The British Roger Moore would not make his debut until decades later.)

So if Joseph, now Roger Moore, was so alienated from his brother Robert, how did he come to participate as an extra in a number of Robert's films? The answer may be that he had little choice. To be successful as an extra, one must be available when called. There is no turning down a small role, credited or not, because it does not appeal to you or because you dislike one of the stars. It's also possible that Joseph and Robert seldom, if ever, saw one another on the set. Joe's brief appearances probably could have been shot on one day, and Bob might have been in the cafeteria or not even on the lot.

Whatever the difficulty was between Robert and Joseph, it apparently never was resolved. Neither Joseph nor Robert ever discussed the matter publicly. Joseph died March 24, 1999, at the age of ninety-eight. There is no record of a funeral being attended by any of his siblings.

———

MEANWHILE, BACK ON THE LOT...

In MGM's 1938 film *Paradise for Three*, Frank Morgan is a wealthy industrialist who checks on his workers by mingling with them incognito. Unemployed Fritz Hagedorn (Robert Young) has eyes for his daughter Hilda (Florence Rice). Reginald Owen is a befuddled butler and Mary Astor is a gold-digging dame. Roger Moore appears uncredited as a telephone operator reporting a fire. Morgan steals the show as a rich guy pretending to be a regular Joe.

Three Comrades (MGM) stars Robert Taylor, Franchot Tone and Robert Young as three friends, former German soldiers, whose comradeship is strengthened by their shared love for the same woman (Margaret Sullavan), who is dying of tuberculosis. Guy Kibbee and Monty Woolley have supporting roles, and Roger Moore appears uncredited as a party guest.

The film is adapted from a novel of the same name by Erich Maria Remarque, author of *All Quiet on the Western Front*. It is another message film, set in a period following World War I, during the Weimar Republic, and deals with the rise of Nazism.

Robert next joined Don Ameche and Simone Simon for the 20th Century-Fox comedy *Josette*, in which two brothers fall in love with the same nightclub singer. Bert Lahr and comedienne Joan Davis add to the comic segments. Lon Chaney Jr. and William Demarest have supporting roles, and Robert Lowery appears uncredited as a boatman.

Don Ameche appeared in many films, including his role as Alexander Graham Bell, about which he was often kidded. He nonetheless is probably best remembered for teaming up with

Francis Langford on the hilarious radio series *The Bickersons*, which aired from 1946 to 1952.

Back at MGM, Robert Young had a supporting role in *The Toy Wife*, starring Luise Rainer and Melvyn Douglas. Rainer is the real star, playing the beautiful but frivolous wife of a plantation owner in antebellum Louisiana. Lillian Randolph (uncredited) plays a Black nun.

The German-born Luise Rainer began her acting career at the age of sixteen. In 1936, after emigrating to America, she had a supporting role in the musical biography *The Great Ziegfeld*, but audiences were so impressed by her emotion-filled performance that she was awarded the Oscar for Best Actress. The following year she played a poor Chinese farm wife in the screen version of novelist Pearl S. Buck's *The Good Earth*, and again she won the award for Best Actress. She was the first thespian to win multiple Academy Awards and the first to win them back-to-back. She and Jodie Foster are the only actresses ever to win two Oscars before the age of thirty.

A footnote about *The Toy Wife*: Robert Young gets to fight a duel with Melvyn Douglas. (Spoiler alert: he loses.)

Robert next costarred with Ruth Hussey and Lew Ayres in MGM's *Rich Man, Poor Girl* (a remake of the 1929 film *The Idle Rich*). A rich businessman wants to marry his secretary, but first he must pass muster with her middle-class family. Lana Turner and Guy Kibbee have supporting roles. MGM was grooming Lana Turner as a star. This was but her second appearance in an MGM film, and she was just seventeen.

The Shining Hour (MGM) stars Joan Crawford and Margaret Sullavan, with Robert Young, Melvyn Douglas, and Hattie McDaniel in supporting roles. Nightclub dancer Olivia (Crawford), seeking a better life, marries well-to-do farmer Henry Linden (Douglas) and joins him on his Wisconsin farm. Henry's brother David (Young), who is married, takes a liking to Olivia, and she finds that she is attracted to him. David's wife, Judy (Sullavan), becomes an ally who tries to help Olivia work things out. Crawford is impressive in a climactic scene involving a fire in the farmhouse.

How she landed
a millionaire

RICH MAN
POOR GIRL
with Robert YOUNG

LEW AYRES · RUTH HUSSEY · GUY KIBBEE
RITA JOHNSON · LANA TURNER
SCREEN PLAY BY JOSEPH A. FIELD
AND JEROME CHODOROV
PRODUCED BY EDWARD CHODOROV
DIRECTED BY REINHOLD SCHUNZEL
A Metro-Goldwyn-Mayer PICTURE

Whatever his qualms about appearing in mostly B pictures, Robert's contract with MGM gave him some reassurance of his ability to provide for his family. That responsibility took on a bit more significance in 1938, when Betty gave birth to their second daughter, Barbara Queen. Carol Anne was now pleased to have a new baby sister.

———

Although he appeared in only nine films over the next two years, MGM was able to keep Robert Young busy without loaning him out to any other studio. Several of his films were notable, even if they were still in the B picture class.

Robert's nagging sense of insecurity might have been eased had he realized at the time how valuable he was to MGM. Producers and directors gave him high marks for being always dependable and reliable. In later years, Bob remarked, only half-jokingly, "When they couldn't get the really big stars, they'd say, 'Okay, then let's get Bob'."

To co-star with dancer Eleanor Powell, Robert got another all-expenses-paid trip to the islands for 1939's *Honolulu*. A famous movie star who yearns for a break from his overzealous fans meets a Hawaiian plantation owner who could be his twin, and trades places with him for a few weeks. Robert played both roles, but received no bonus check.

The film is notable for a number of other well known performers who play supporting and minor roles, including Ruth Hussey, Eleanor Powell, and Eddie Anderson, best known as Jack Benny's sassy butler Rochester. George Burns and Gracie Allen each play separate roles until one brief scene when they do a bit of their shtick. The Pied Pipers, joined by Jo Stafford, perform uncredited. In a comic musical scene featuring Gracie Allen, some musicians and people in the audience are made up to look like the Marx Brothers, Clark Gable, W. C. Fields and Oliver Hardy.

Although she shared top billing with Young, the film's real star is the lovely and talented dancer Eleanor Powell. In an elaborate nightclub scene, surrounded by about forty female hula dancers, and wearing an outfit that shows a lot of flesh, she does a number that is described in the MGM preview trailer as "the most amazing dance routine of the decade!" In another scene, she performs a remarkable tap dance number intended as a tribute to the renowned Bill "Bojangles" Robinson, in top hat and blackface. Unfortunately, although not unusual at the time, such a production is understandably reviled today.

Robert got to play another rich guy in *Bridal Suite*, costarring with Annabelle (no last name). The French-born actress no doubt felt that her birth name, Suzanne Georgette Charpentier, was too lengthy, and elected to perform under a memorable single moniker. (Hey, it worked for Sabu and Madonna.)

This time, Robert plays a spoiled young playboy who finds true love when circumstances require him to do actual work in a Swiss chalet. Supporting players include Gene Lockhart, Arthur Treacher, Billie Burke and Walter Connolly. Appearing uncredited is a very young Robert Blake, who would later star in the 1970s television series *Baretta*.

Ever the gentleman, Robert once again took a back seat to his co-star, Ann Sothern, in *Maisie*. Based on a series of short stories by Nell Martin, it spotlights a brash but lovable Brooklyn showgirl named Maisie Ravier. MGM bought the rights to bring the character to the screen and planned to use Carole Lombard as the star. Married to Clark Gable, Lombard was a lovely actress with a flair for the screwball comedy genre. Sadly, before a script was completed, she died in a TWA plane crash. She was but thirty-three years old.

MGM then selected Sothern to fill the role, and she proved to be a perfect Maisie. The film was such a hit that it spawned a successful series of nine sequels, with such titles as *Congo Maisie*, *Gold Rush Maisie*, and *Up Goes Maisie*. Sothern parlayed their popularity into a network radio series, *The Adventures of Maisie*, that ran from 1945 to 1947 on CBS. Her frequently uttered "Likewise, I'm sure" became a catchphrase for her many fans.

In *Miracles for Sale,* Robert Young plays Mike Morgan, a magician whose sideline is exposing fraudulent magicians and psychics who prey on the unsuspecting. Florence Rice is Judy Barclay, a young woman whose life is in danger, and Morgan is trying to figure out why. When a noted demonologist is murdered, Mike assists the police in developing suspects, who include two magicians, a couple who perform tricks by telepathy, and a psychic. The film is filled with twists and turns that are both mysterious and comic.

William Demarest, who played Uncle Charley on the television series *My Three Sons*, appears as a detective. Roger Moore (uncredited) is a volunteer at a magic show.

Truman Bradley (also uncredited), appears as a nightclub master of ceremonies. Bradley began his career in the 1930s, working as a radio broadcaster and news commentator at Chicago's station WBBM. With his distinctive, authoritative voice, he soon became a radio actor as well as a narrator in numerous movies. During the 1950s, he was the host of the syndicated television series *Science Fiction Theatre*.

As the decade came to an end, Robert still had the security of a contract with Metro-Goldwyn-Mayer, but he felt that he was underused. The B pictures that continually relied upon him generally took at most four weeks to film. Those with few set changes could sometimes be finished in three weeks or less. Some time was spent prior to filming in reading and memorizing scripts, but overall he was not being overworked.

A homebody by nature, he was pleased to have time to spend with his family. Still, a steady paycheck did not by itself give a sense of fulfillment and success. His frustration, kept mostly bottled up within, was building toward troubles that would weigh heavily upon him down the road.

Radio Days

Robert Young on the air at NBC; *Nostalgia Digest collection*

Near the end of the 1930s, that marvelous medium called radio was coming into its own. During the Great Depression, it had provided a great source of comfort to struggling families. Whether on a store-bought receiver or a homemade crystal set, they could tune in to hours of information and entertainment at no cost other than a few pennies' worth of electricity.

Early on, other than in large cities, most programs emanated from small nearby stations whose broadcast towers had a limited range. Almost everything aired was by local talent, although some music was provided by traveling musicians and singers.

When radio's electronic wizards determined how to connect stations, networking began. By the late 1930s, networks had made radio a truly commercial enterprise. The National Broadcasting Company and the Columbia Broadcasting System were providing programs nationwide, and the American Broadcasting Company would soon follow. Stations in small towns and rural areas could now pick up and offer their listeners programs that originated from network stations in Los Angeles, New York City, Chicago and other large cities. As the variety and quality of programming expanded and improved, the 1940s would one day be referred to as The Golden Age of Radio.

In the last years of the Depression, this free entertainment might have seemed a threat to the film industry, but Hollywood saw it differently. People still yearned for an occasional escape from the hard times, and the cost of a movie was minimal. Filmmakers sought ways to utilize radio to attract more people into the theaters.

As early as November, 1937, Metro-Goldwyn-Mayer launched a program called *Good News of 1937* (with the year updated in 1938 and 1939). Each week the studio presented a radio adaptation of one of its films, with the original stars filling their film roles. In opening announcements, Maxwell House Coffee was the official sponsor, and paid $25,000 per week for the privilege. But lest anyone fail to note what studio was providing this entertainment, the program began with the familiar roar of the MGM lion.

Until it was phased out in early 1940, *Good News* presented a potpourri of romantic dramas, mysteries, musicals, and comedies. Unlike its counterpart, *Lux Radio Theatre*, which adapted films from all major studios, *Good News* adapted only MGM films, thus promoting the films and helping to glamorize the male and female stars.

On one program, Robert Young was joined by actress Joan Crawford for a romantic sketch called "The Moon Is On Fire." Young also had the distinction of being chosen to host *Good News* for the 1938-1939 season. He was in good company, following in the footsteps of James Stewart and Robert Taylor.

With the United States' entry into World War II, NBC launched its *Victory Parade* program. Produced in cooperation with the Office of War Information, the program presented wartime messages and promoted the sale of war bonds in lieu of the usual commercials. Each weekly program drew from NBC's nightly prime-time lineup, including such stars as Red Skelton, Rudy Vallee, Edgar Bergen and Charlie McCarthy, Fibber McGee and Molly, Bob Hope, and Jack Benny, as well as such programs as *Mr. District Attorney*; *The Aldrich Family*, and novelties such as *Truth or Consequences* and *Kay Kyser's Kollege of Musical Knowledge*. On a night featuring *The Screen Guild Theatre*, Robert Young and Ruth Hussey starred in a presentation of the play *Joe Smith, American*. Robert would later reprise his role in a screen adaptation of the play.

Beginning in 1941 and running through early 1946, an NBC program called *The Open House* was presented as a musical variety/interview program. It was mostly a showcase for singer Helen Morgan, but hostess Ona Munson interviewed such Hollywood stars as Groucho Marx, Billie Burke, Ruth Hussey, Robert Young and others. She focused on human interest stories and presented the stars as "real people." Groucho Marx? Maybe. But Robert Young certainly qualified.

In 1943, Robert was cast in his first starring role in a continuing radio drama. At the request of the Office of War Information, CBS recruited renowned writer Norman Corwin to create a "goodwill" documentary series about the fighting countries of the United Nations. In *Passport for Adams*, Young plays newsman

Doug Adams, who is sent on a world tour to see how ordinary people live in other countries. Adams is selected for the mission because of his small-town background on the premise that "most of the people of the world are small-town people."

Adams is accompanied by photographer Perry "Quiz" Quisinberry, played by Dane Clark. Quiz frequently has questions or judgmental reactions to people they encounter. In response, Adams would enlighten him about local customs and difficulties of daily life that were unknown to folks back in the land of the free. In the process, he imparted information to the radio listener.

In August of 1944, NBC premiered *The Frank Morgan Show*. It was a variety show that mostly featured Morgan (the wizard in MGM's *Wizard of Oz*) as a teller of tall–*really* tall–tales. Comedienne Cass Daley came along for the ride. Harlow Wilcox, long-time announcer on *Fibber McGee and Molly*, filled that role. Somehow Robert Young was selected to be the host of the program, which also required him to serve as Morgan's straight man. The show lasted but one season.

In June, 1944, CBS began a series called *The Doctor Fights*. It was sponsored by Schenley Laboratories, one of twenty-two companies that had taken on the production of penicillin. Its dual purpose was to acquaint the public with the new miracle drug and to honor the 60,000 doctors who were serving in theaters of war. Each episode told a true story involving a real doctor on the field of battle. One recalled a doctor keeping patients in a Japanese prison camp alive "to fight another day." Another involved the wrenching dilemma of a medical officer faced with using his dwindling supply of penicillin to treat German prisoners.

Playing the principal role each week, Robert Young took turns with Ronald Colman, Robert Cummings, Van Heflin, Gene Lockhart, Robert Montgomery, and Vincent Price. Again, he was in good company.

Likewise in 1947, when he alternated with such stars as Marlene Dietrich, Charles Laughton, James Mason, and Franchot Tone on the short-lived *Studio One*. The program presented adaptations of plays and books rendered as close as possible to their original content in the time allotted. At the end of each program, actors came forward to give their names along with what part they played, thus building listener identification.

The show was highly praised by press reviewers, but it aired opposite *Fibber McGee and Molly* and *The Bob Hope Show*. Against such stiff competition, its fate was foreordained, and it lasted but one season.

In 1948, Norman Corwin left CBS and joined United Nations Radio. There, in 1950, he produced one of his most powerful radio dramas. Aired on the Mutual Broadcasting System, *Document A/777* involved a roll call vote in the U.N. General Assembly for a proposed "International Bill of Human Rights." As the voting proceeds, the action freezes for some countries while incidents from their past are dramatized. Some brutal warlords and dictatorial leaders are exposed in these historical dramatizations.

Representatives of the Assembly were portrayed by a formidable cast that included Charles Boyer, Lee J. Cobb, Ronald Colman, Joan Crawford, Van Heflin, Jean Hersholt, Lena Horn, Charles Laughton, Laurence Olivier, Edward G. Robinson and many others. In what must have seemed a place of honor, Robert Young assumed the role of the person calling the roll.

During radio's heyday in the 1940s and early 1950s, countless screen stars appeared as guests on comedy, variety, musical and dramatic radio programs. Many top stars took on their own series. Comedians Red Skelton and Bob Hope, crooner Bing Crosby, and singer/comic Eddie Cantor had long-running weekly shows. Marie Wilson became *My Friend Irma*, Eve Arden was *Our Miss Brooks*, and Fanny Brice was hilariously annoying as the bratty *Baby Snooks*. Humphrey Bogart was Slate Shannon on *Bold Venture* and James Stewart was a Western hero on *Six Shooter*.

In the popular detective genre, Dick Powell did double duty, first as Richard Rogue in *Rogue's Gallery*, and later as *Richard Diamond, Private Detective*. On the latter series, the writers often found an opportunity to pause the action as Powell sang a song to his secretary.

Top box office stars usually were able to produce their own programs and enjoy the financial benefits thereof. When the Western series *Six Shooter* aired, James Stewart was both producer and star, in effect owning the program.

Minor stars and supporting players generally were farmed out to various radio programs much as they were to other studios. Whatever fee was negotiated with the network or sponsor went to the players' studios. The fee always was more than the players would be receiving on their weekly check from the studio. The studios thus reaped a profit from their contract players even if they had no current film roles for them.

Radio appearances afforded a means of mentioning actors' and actresses' names to listeners between pictures, and the studio names were always mentioned. When Dick Powell had a film currently making the rounds, the announcer's closing comments often would include a mention that "Dick Powell may currently be seen in…" If he had recently finished a film yet to be released, the announcer would say, "Dick Powell may soon be seen in…"

In addition to the programs on which he appeared regularly, Robert Young made frequent guest appearances on such programs as *Kraft Music Hall, The Lady Esther Screen Guild Players, Suspense, Lux Radio Theatre, Family Theatre,* and several *Cavalcade of America* episodes, as well as thirty appearances on *The Gulf Screen Guild Theatre*. In 1941, he starred in a radio adaptation of Zane Grey's novel *Western Union* on *The Kate Smith Radio Hour*.

Except for his role in *Passport for Adams,* which lasted but one season, Robert Young's radio appearances were not such as to earn him any devoted fans who were not already impressed by his screen roles. Nevertheless, they made him a seasoned performer in the medium, which was to be a major benefit later in his career.

———

Robert Young
in Paramount Pictures
P2025-N

1940S: TURMOIL AND TRANSITION

America was not yet in the war as the 1940s began, but it was becoming increasingly clear that the nation would eventually be drawn in. Military preparations were underway, and many wartime supplies were being furnished to our friends in Great Britain.

Despite apprehensions, life went on, and at a more exhilarating pace as the country slowly revived from the Depression's impact. Theater owners who had suffered sparse attendance began to see seats nearly filled again. Moviegoers seeking both entertainment and an escape from the troubling news of the day were ripe for new screen attractions. Hollywood was pleased to oblige.

Robert Young began the new decade costarring with Spencer Tracy and Walter Brennan in MGM's *Northwest Passage*. The epic Western has Langdon Towne (Young) and 'Hunk' Marriner (Brennan) joining Major Robert Rogers (Tracy) in 1759 for a grueling expedition, hindered by a fierce Indian tribe, as they seek a northwest passage to the Pacific.

There's much horsing around in *Florian* (MGM), loosely based on the book by Felix Salten (author of *Bambi*). Anton (Young), a groom who cares for the Lippizaner stallion Florian, owned by Archduke Oliver (Lee Bowman), becomes romantically attached to the archduke's daughter Diana (Helen Gilbert). The story focuses mostly on a series of unfortunate incidents that have the great horse passing from owner to owner, some less than kind. It takes a journey all the way to New York, but eventually horse and lovers are reunited.

Joined by Maureen O'Sullivan, and Lewis Stone, Robert next starred in another horse tale, MGM's *Sporting Blood*. While training his horse for an upcoming Virginia stakes race, Myles Vanders (Young) has a feud with neighbor Davis Lockwood (Stone). That becomes inconvenient when he falls in love with Vanders' daughter Linda (O'Sullivan). All ends well when he wins the race and Linda's heart.

With Margaret Sullavan and James Stewart in the starring roles, Robert was teamed with Robert Stack, Frank Morgan, Dan Dailey and Ward Bond in MGM's *The Mortal Storm*. The Roth family is living a quiet life in the German Alps. The tense drama has the family torn apart in the turmoil of 1933 when Adolf Hitler becomes Chancellor of Germany and his fascist followers gain control of the country.

Based on a 1937 book of the same title, *The Mortal Storm* was one of many anti-Nazi films that Hollywood began producing even before America entered the war. Hitler was familiar with the book. Furious when he learned that it was being adapted to the screen, he added the names of all the cast members to his infamous "death list."

Robert Young took the threat seriously and was quite disturbed. Robert Stack recalled years later that between takes in the filming Robert was observed walking nervously around the studio and muttering to himself, "What will become of my family?"

In Young's next film, MGM's *Dr. Kildare's Crisis*, Robert is the cause of the good doctor's problem. Lew Ayres plays the young doctor in this sixth film in the series, with Lionel Barrymore as his older companion and mentor, Dr. Leonard Gillespie. Kildare has become engaged to Mary Lamont (Laraine Day), and the wedding date is drawing near. Then Mary's brother Douglas (Young) begins suffering seizures, and the diagnosis is hereditary epilepsy. Mary decides that she must forgo marriage and care for her brother. Tune in tomorrow...

Robert could now chalk up a decade of steady film work, even though his output had been lean in some years. Nevertheless, he was plagued with doubts about his future. He began most days entering the lot bracing himself for comments from various folks. Picking up on Louis B. Mayer's comment, one might say, "Gee, Bob, if only you could put on a little more weight." Another might observe with a grin, "Gee, Bob, if only you had some sex appeal."

These were friends who were simply joking with him. Robert knew that, but although he might grin in response, their jibes stirred a dark foreboding in him. Many years later, he explained that "I was an introvert in an extrovert profession," and went on to confess, "All those years at MGM I hid a black terror behind a cheerful face."

Dr. KILDARE'S CRISIS
A Metro-Goldwyn-Mayer Picture
Case No. 6
THE RIDDLE OF WHISPERING WOMEN!
with
LEW AYRES ★ LIONEL BARRYMORE
LARAINE DAY ★ ROBERT YOUNG
And the Guest Star
Screen Play by Harry Ruskin and Willis Goldbeck
Directed by HAROLD S. BUCQUET
A Metro-Goldwyn-Mayer Picture

For his first film of 1941, Robert Young joined Randolph Scott, and Dean Jagger in the 20th Century-Fox adaptation of a Zane Grey novel, *Western Union*. While leading the construction of Western Union lines to connect East with West, Edward Creighton (Jagger) hires a reformed outlaw, Vance Shaw (Scott) and a tenderfoot Eastern surveyor, Richard Blake (Young). Their efforts are hampered by disgruntled members of Shaw's former gang and Indians distrusting of the white man's mysterious wire. A high-strung drama with some beautiful Arizona backgrounds.

Taking its title from a song, MGM's *Lady Be Good* was a musical-romance starring dancer Eleanor Powell, Ann Sothern, Robert Young, Lionel Barrymore and Red Skelton. Tom Conway, Dan Dailey and Phil Silvers have supporting roles. Connie Russell and Doris Day both contribute songs but don't yet rate having their names in the credits. Red Skelton provides some laughs as Joe "Red" Willet. Robert Young even gets to do a little singing.

Composer Eddie Crane (Young) and his lyricist wife Dixie (Sothern) are a successful team writing hit Broadway shows, but their marriage is becoming a sour note. Can they get it retuned before the finale?

Eleanor Powell received top billing because of her popularity and her excellent dance numbers. In a sequence directed by Busby Berkeley, she dances through a long series of pianos as off-camera stage hands remove the ones she has passed. In another delightful set, she does a dance routine with a dog she has trained especially for the number.

In MGM's *Married Bachelor*, con man Randy Haven (Robert Young) accepts an unpublished manuscript about bachelorhood in payment for the author's gambling debt. When he succeeds in having it published and it becomes a best seller, he must pretend to be single. This doesn't sit well with his wife Norma (Ruth Hussey). Lee Bowman and Sheldon Leonard have supporting roles.

Sheldon Leonard may be best remembered as bartender Nick in *It's a Wonderful Life*. He had the face, voice, and build of a tough guy or gangster and played that part in many films. On radio, he frequently showed up as a multi-talented tout on *The Jack Benny Show*. Jack would be at a railroad depot, a furniture store, or whatever, and Leonard would say: "Psst! Hey, Bud. C'mere a minute." After asking what Benny was planning to purchase, he would say, "Uh, uh!" and talk him out of it with goofy and hilarious logic. "Dat engine slows on da curves." Or: "Look at the skinny legs on dat table." The routine was so popular that Leonard tagged along when Jack took his show to television.

Robert next starred with Hedy Lamarr and Ruth Hussey in MGM's *H. M. Pulham, Esq.* Middle-aged businessman Harry Pelham (Young) has lived a contented but very conservative life with his wife Kay (Hussey). Organizing a twenty-five-year college reunion causes him to reminisce about a brief romance with the free-spirited Marvin Miles (Lamarr). Seeing her again at the reunion, he comes to realize what a good woman he has in Kay.

Bonita Granville, Van Heflin and Charles Coburn have supporting roles. A young Ava Gardner appears uncredited.

———

As 1942 began, Americans were faced with a grim and frightening reality. On the previous December 7th, the Japanese had made an unprovoked and deadly attack upon the United States at the Navy's Pearl Harbor base in Hawaii. President Franklin D. Roosevelt had addressed Congress and the nation with a declaration of war. Young men across the country were signing up for military service. Plants large and small were retooling from whatever their commercial products had been to begin producing weapons of war.

Hollywood shifted gears to begin participating in the war effort. Some stars, including Gene Autry, Clark Gable, William Holden, Burt Lancaster, Audey Murphy, David Niven, Tyrone Power and James Stewart, enlisted in various services.

Other stars began putting on shows for the boys at various camps. Bands and singers provided music. Comedians did their routines, often incorporating gags that were relevant to the service group or camp where they were performing. Many of Bob Hope's radio broadcasts were "remotes" from camps, and he closed each show by telling the listening audience: "Bye, bye, and buy bonds." Always the shows included appearances by some of Hollywood's beautiful female stars and upcoming starlets.

In 1942, taking a cue from the USO clubs around the country, the film folk opened the Hollywood Canteen. Meals were free, with male stars working as waiters (only soft drinks served) and in the kitchen. The bands of Duke Ellington, Glenn Miller, the Dorsey brothers and others provided music. The GIs got to dance with Hedy Lamarr, Betty Grable, June Allyson, Alice Faye and numerous young lovelies waiting to be discovered.

Meanwhile the studios began producing many films with military and patriotic themes.

MGM's *Joe Smith, American* is a perfect example. Robert Young is Joe, a worker in an aircraft plant where a top secret bombsight is being developed. After seeing the plans just once,

Joe demonstrates that he can redraw them from memory, and he is put in charge of the project. Enemy agents get wind of this. They kidnap Joe, blindfold him, and take him to a remote hideout. There they beat him mercilessly, but even when it seems he may die of his torture, he refuses to reproduce the plans. Miraculously, when his captors leave him alone, he manages to escape. His uncanny memory provides a string of tiny clues that enable the FBI to track down and capture his kidnappers.

"You're prettier than when we were married. I'm certainly a lucky guy!"

Marsha Hunt plays Joe's wife Mary. A young Darryl Hickman plays their son Johnny. Connie Russel has another uncredited supporting role.

In the opening credits of the film, a scrolling message says: "This story is about a man who defended his country. His name is Joe Smith. He is an American. This picture is a tribute to all Joe Smiths."

One reviewer noted that Robert seemed to have a face and personality most suited for comedy or romantic dramas, but felt that he was quite effective as an honest everyman whose intelligence and bravery bring down the enemy agents. A *Newsweek* reviewer said, "The acting—particularly Robert Young in the title role—is unaffected and credible."

Another man named Smith is the hero of the simply-titled *Cairo*. Robert costars with the lovely Jeanette MacDonald in her last film while under contract with MGM. The film was billed as a musical comedy, but its primary plot is not light-hearted. Newspaper reporter Homer Smith (Young) suspects that actress Marcia Warren (MacDonald) is a Nazi spy. While she is "between pictures" in London, he cons his way into being hired as her butler. After concluding that he is mistaken, he joins forces with Marcia and her maid to bring down the real Nazis, who are plotting to bomb Allied convoys with remote-controlled planes.

Two of Hollywood's best known Black stars appear in supporting roles. The popular jazz, swing, and blues singer Ethel Waters plays Marcia's maid, Cleona. Dooley Wilson plays a fellow named Hector who has a crush on Cleona. Wilson probably is best remembered as Sam, the nightclub piano player, who sings "As Time Goes By" in the classic film *Casablanca.* Film buffs will most likely remember MacDonald for the films in which she costarred with Nelson Eddy and the two sang romantic duets.

Set in London during World War II, MGM's *Journey for Margaret* stars Robert Young and Laraine Day as a couple who have to deal with the loss of their unborn child due to a bombing raid. American war correspondent John Davis (Young) and his pregnant wife Nora (Day) are in London during the Blitz. John is surveying the ruins after a raid when he learns that Nora has been injured and taken to hospital. They are both devastated by the loss of the unborn baby. Later, visiting a shelter for homeless orphans, they fall in love with a girl named Margaret (Margaret O'Brien). They overcome some difficulties to adopt her, but then must deal with even more challenging obstacles getting her out of London to accompany them back home to Connecticut.

Robert's secret feelings of insecurity persisted, even though he seemed to have become a fixture at Metro-Goldwyn-Mayer. He confessed years later that he was haunted by a secret sense that he was a failure. Having a long-term contract did not prevent him from forever worrying about whether he could adequately provide for his family.

His work in 1942 was some consolation. Even if they were considered B pictures, *Joe Smith, American* and *Journey for Margaret* were two of his most powerful and memorable films.

———

Robert Young began 1943 on a more light-hearted note. Loaned out to 20th Century-Fox, he joined Dorothy McGuire, Ina Claire, Reginald Gardiner, Olga Baclanova, and Jean Howard in the comedy-drama *Claudia*, based on a 1941 Broadway play of the same name. David Naughton (Young) is finding his married life difficult because his child bride Claudia (McGuire), transported to his remote farm, can't stand living far from her mother. She also believes that her husband doesn't find her desirable enough. She tries to make him jealous by flirting with a neighbor. Then, to force a move back to the city, she secretly sells the farm. (Wasn't his name on the deed? Oh, well.) Fortunately, Claudia matures impressively when she discovers that she is pregnant.

Back home at MGM, Robert next starred with Lana Turner and Walter Brennan in the romantic comedy *Slightly Dangerous*. Turner is Peggy Evans, a bored young woman in a dead-end job who has a freak accident that enables her to pose as Carol Burden, the long-lost daughter of millionaire Cornelius Burden (Brennan). Trouble is, she has to dodge her former boss, Bob Stuart (Young), who won't be fooled by her new hairdo and outfit.

Alan Mowbray has a supporting role as an English gentleman (typecasting?). A very young Robert Blake is seen as a boy on a porch, Cathy Lewis as a salesgirl, and Roger Moore as a floorwalker, all uncredited.

Playing opposite Lana Turner was a bit of a feather in the cap for Robert Young. In the mid-1940s she was at the peak of her popularity and one of Hollywood's highest paid actresses. Being "discovered" while sitting at a soda fountain became the fantasy of thousands of teenage girls, and women everywhere sought to replicate the provocative bang that hung over her left eye.

Robert next again walked across the street to 20th Century-Fox to join Betty Grable, Adolphe Menjou, Virginia Grey, and Reginald Gardiner in the Technicolor musical *Sweet Rosie O'Grady*. To improve her status and better herself, burlesque performer Rosie O'Grady (Grable) moves to London, becomes a musical comedy star under the name Madeleine Marlowe, and gets engaged to Charles, Duke of Trippingham (Gardiner). Things start to unravel when American reporter Sam Magee (Young) exposes her, not on stage, but on the front page. It should be no news flash that their clash leads to a re-engagement.

Betty Grable had just recently starred in the film *Coney Island,* which was an enormous success. *Coney Island* and *Sweet Rosie O'Grady* were two of 20th Century-Fox's big money makers in 1943, and were among the top ten high-grossing films of the year. With studios sending stars' photos to anyone who asked for them, Grable became one of the top pin-up girls for servicemen at home and over there.

As 1944 began, much of the world was still in turmoil as World War II raged on, but hard-fought Allied victories gave hope that the enemies would soon be defeated. Americans on the home front participated in various facets of the war effort and went about their lives with as much normalcy as possible, enduring rationing, shortages and other difficulties. Hollywood continued to crank out films that would provide both entertainment and brief escape.

Robert Young joined Charles Laughton, Margaret O'Brien, William Gargan and Peter Lawford in MGM's *The Canterville Ghost*. In the fantasy-comedy based on a short story by Oscar Wilde, the ghost of Sir Simon de Canterville (Laughton) is condemned to haunt the family's English castle until some descendant restores the family honor with an act of bravery. Centuries later, Cuffy Williams (Young), an American soldier stationed near the castle, is befriended by six-year-old Lady Jessica (O'Brien) and learns that he is distantly related to Sir Simon. Unfortunately, Williams is low on courage and has managed to be assigned to duty that normally does not require it. But fate provides the opportunity and Lady Jessica provides the encouragement that enables him to save his comrades from a disaster and free Sir Simon's ghost.

The perky Margaret O'Brien is just right for her role as Williams' encourager. William Gargan appears as Sergeant Benson and Peter Lawford (later of the Sinatra rat pack) is Anthony de Canterville.

The Canterville Ghost was to be Robert Young's only film in 1944. His contract with Metro Goldwyn Mayer would soon be up for renewal. The MGM brass, which must by then have considered him like one of the family, was ready to make an offer and prepare the paperwork. But when they approached Bob he declined.

Having been a faithful servant for more than a decade, and still delegated to roles for minor stars, he had determined to step out on his own and seek more fulfilling opportunities. Many years later, in an interview with film critic Leonard Maltin, Robert said he had discussed with Betty the prospect of him freelancing. As always, Betty urged him to do what he thought best.

"All those guys [Hollywood stars] went to serve in the war," he told Maltin, "my career didn't change, and now they're coming back. If it didn't change with them away, it's not gonna change with them back. I think I can do better on the outside by myself, freelancing."

There is no record of Bob's meeting with the bosses, but it's likely that he was almost apologetic in turning them down. Accepting his last check, Robert Young departed the Metro-Goldwyn-Mayer lot.

His decision may also have been prompted by another blessed event on the home front. That year, Elizabeth gave birth to their third daughter, Elizabeth Louise. Family man Bob now had one more reason to look out for those nearest and dearest to him. Thank goodness for those four bedrooms.

———

Freelancing is a risky business in almost any profession. In addition to providing a good — if not superior — product, it requires selling one's self. For all his hidden insecurity difficulties, Robert Young knew his way around Hollywood. He had worked satisfactorily for all of the major studios. He had never given any directors reason to dislike him and was friends with many of the people on the studio crews.

Moreover, he had become friends with many of the actors and actresses with whom he had appeared in various films. Having spread the word that he was available, many of these folk might suggest to a producer or director that he was right for some new role. He also was able to negotiate a five-year agreement with RKO Radio Pictures that called for them to use him in at least one film per year.

One uplifting result of that agreement was 1945's *The Enchanted Cottage,* in which he starred with Dorothy McGuire, Herbert Marshall, and Mildred Natwick. It was one of his most memorable films and one for which he had the most satisfying recollections.

Pilot Oliver Bradford (Young) is disfigured by war wounds and flees from family and friends to a seaside New England cottage that he rents from a Mrs. Minnett (Natwick). He is befriended by a blind pianist (Marshall) who lives nearby, but shuns other contacts. He must, however, endure the frequent presence of Laura Pennington (McGuire), a shy, homely woman hired by Mrs. Minnett as the cottage's housekeeper.

As the two come to know one another, they each become more attractive in the other's eyes. A gradual transformation takes place, facilitated by the film's makeup crew, and visible to no one other than the couple themselves and the movie audience. Oliver and Laura come to believe that the cottage is enchanted as their eyes are opened to each other's inner beauty.

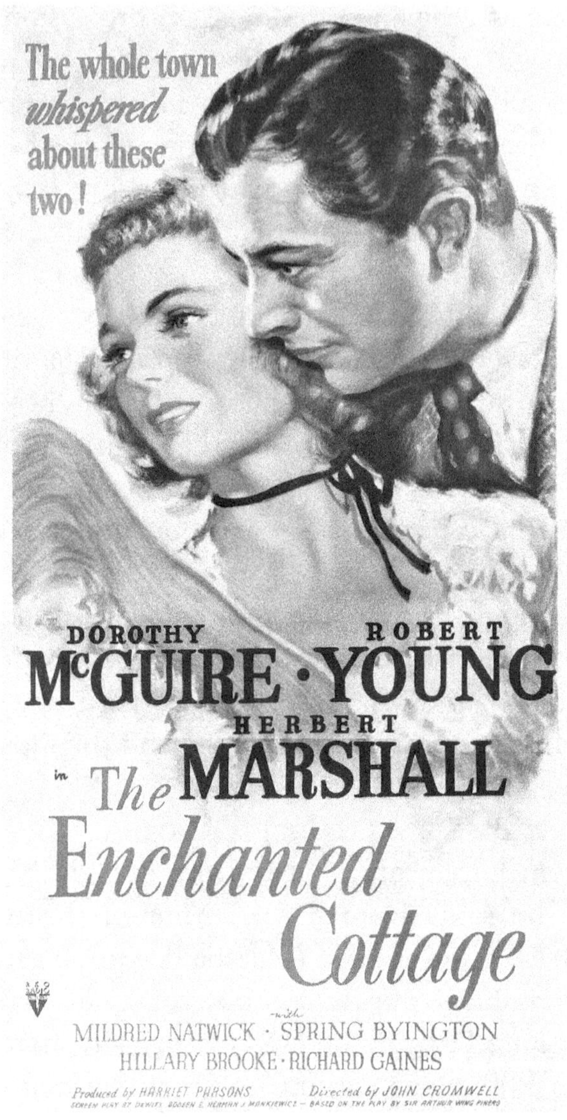

RKO utilized Robert again in 1945 for *Those Endearing Young Charms*, a comedy film in which he starred with Laraine Day, Ann Harding, and Bill Williams. In 1945, Helen Brandt (Day) is dating Jerry (Williams), an Army private home on leave. She considers him just a friend, but when he introduces her to his buddy, Lt. Hurley 'Hank' Travers (Young), she is smitten. A romance begins, but Jerry warns her that Hank has a reputation as a love-

'em-and-leave-'em guy. Then her mother (Harding) confesses to losing her first love before marrying her father. Hank has told her that this time he's serious. As the boys prepare to return to base, she must decide if she can risk giving him her heart.

In 1946, Dorothy McGuire and Robert Young were paired again as 20th Century-Fox called upon them to reprise their roles from the film *Claudia*. In *Claudia and David,* a subplot involves jealousy surrounding David Naughton (Young) consulting on a building project with Elizabeth Van Doren (Mary Astor) and the uninvited attentions of married neighbor Phil Dexter (John Sutton) toward Claudia Naughton (McGuire).

The main story, however, deals with the Naughtons' differing views on raising their three-year-old son Bobby (Anthony Sydes). They both love him dearly, but David tends to be strict and believes Claudia coddles him too much, while Claudia believes David is too wrapped up in his work to give their son enough attention. Their parenting differences and the other issues put a strain on what had been a serene marriage.

Speaking of the film version of *Claudia* and its sequel some years later, Young said of his co-star, "She'd done it on Broadway and this was mostly a photographed play. Ina Claire was wonderful as her mother. It did sensational business, and Fox requested a sequel. Dorothy was aghast, and said she'd never do a sequel; but technically, she was under contract to Selznick. He simply put his foot down and *Claudia and David* duly appeared in 1946 and was almost as big a hit."

Recruited by Paramount Pictures, Robert next starred in *The Searching Wind* with Sylvia Sidney, and Ann Richards. Alex Hazen, a career diplomat, is reluctant to take sides as troubles brew in Europe in the 1920s and 1930s. He is romantically involved with Cassie Bowman (Sidney), who urges him to return to America. When he declines, she leaves without him. He meets, woos and marries Emily Hazen (Richards). When World War II breaks out, he relents and they leave. In 1945, they have a dinner party with their son Sam (Douglas Dick), recently returned from the war, and guest Cassie. When they hear a radio announcement that Mussolini has been killed, all that went before is reviewed as Alex reflects upon mistakes he made during his diplomatic career.

The film originally was to have been produced by Hal Wallis at Warner Bros., but Wallis left the Warners and brought the project to Paramount. One notable feature of the film is a segment of archive footage in which President Franklin D. Roosevelt speaks, as himself, but uncredited.

In the RKO Radio Pictures nonsensical comedy film *Lady Luck*, Robert Young stars with Barbara Hale and Frank Morgan.

Mary Audrey (Hale), who hates gambling, puts her grandfather, William (Morgan), to work in her Beverly Hills bookstore to keep him occupied. Gramps nevertheless loses a $200 wager to professional gambler Larry Scott (Young). Larry meets Mary at the store, romance blooms, and they are wed. Without admitting how he earns his income, Larry takes his bride to Las Vegas on their honeymoon. In a bit of Damon Runyon-style nonsense, he persuades her to try playing blackjack "just once" after conniving with the management to let her win $500. Things get wacky when she gets really lucky and wins a bundle. Upon their return home, Larry finds that Gramps not only has kept the bookstore running but now has a little bookmaking operation on the side.

Three films in one year was not bad for someone who was freelancing. There had been years when his MGM contract had resulted in no more, and a couple of years with fewer. The *Canterville Ghost* had been his only film in 1944.

Nevertheless, 1946 was a critical year for Robert Young. His chronic insecurity had at last induced him to seek medical help, and he was diagnosed as suffering from depression. It's most probable that the condition had existed for some time.

Depression was a little understood ailment in the 1940s. It was a subject generally not discussed among family, friends, or associates, in part because of its scary and unexplained nature. Those who suffered from it tended not to acknowledge it, and often avoided seeking help out of embarrassment or fear of knowing what was wrong.

Having been a shy youth by nature, Robert may have been affected to some degree by the mysterious disappearance of his father. A Harvard research study in more recent times found that "significant stress in early childhood…can result in hypertension…with increased potential for fear and anxiety."

In Robert's case, medication was prescribed. It would eventually come to exacerbate the problem when it was determined that he had developed a drug dependency. Initially, however, a diagnosis of the problem, his acceptance of it, and the prescription of a medication, gave him some relief.

Meanwhile, there was some offsetting joy in the birth of the Young's fourth daughter, Kathleen Joy. Someone would now have to share a bedroom with the newcomer.

———

In a rare casting by RKO, Robert Young plays an unsavory fellow in 1947's *They Won't Believe Me*. On trial for murdering his girlfriend, Larry Ballentine (Young) tells the jury a story they may find hard to swallow. While he is cheating on his wealthy wife, Greta (Rita Johnson), Larry's girlfriend Verna Carlson (Susan Hayward) is killed in a fiery car crash. Then his wife, learning of his infidelity, throws herself off a cliff. Since Verna has committed embezzlement in order to run away with Larry, the jury is going to have a hard time accepting his plea of innocence.

Serious film buffs often point out flaws in continuity, background or whatever; things that we casual moviegoers seldom notice. One reviewer noted that in the car crash scene, the car's windshield shatters an instant before the actual crash. He referred to it as a "premature impactulation."

Generally, the film received favorable reviews. One reviewer called the film "An outstanding noir melodrama whose adultery tale is much in the same nature as *Double Indemnity*," the film based on James M. Cain's gritty novel. Another also compared the film to Cain's writing and praised the acting, noting that "Cast against type, Robert Young manages to be both creepy and sympathetic."

Nevertheless, the film was not a money-maker. Speaking of it during an appearance on television's *The Dick Cavett Show* in 1968, Young observed that he had made just one picture in which he played a nasty character, and it resulted in a box-office flop.

Once more at RKO Radio Pictures, Robert starred with Robert Mitchum, Robert Ryan, and Gloria Grahame in *Crossfire*. A man is murdered after a brief, seemingly innocent meeting with a group of recently demobilized soldiers in a bar. Capt. Finlay (Young) and Sgt. Peter Keeley (Mitchum) interview the group, which includes "Monty" Montgomery (Ryan), and a girl who was at the bar, Ginny Tremaine (Grahame). As Finlay and Keeley piece together fragments of the evening from each of those questioned, it begins to appear that the man was killed because he was a Jew.

This was one of several films of the era that involved the troubling issue of anti-Semitism. *Gentlemen's Agreement*, starring Gregory Peck, dealt with the same subject and won the award for Best Picture. Although it did not win, *Crossfire* also was nominated, the first B picture to earn that distinction. The film garnered five nominations in all, two of them earned by Gloria Grahame for Best Supporting Actress and Robert Ryan for Best Supporting Actor. It was RKO's highest grossing film of the year.

When production of the film began, Dick Powell had been selected to play the lead role of Capt. Finlay, but a scheduling conflict caused him to drop out. Not for the first time, Robert Young was tapped to fill a vacancy, and he gave one of his most powerful performances. He was gratified to play the role and said that *Crossfire* deserved credit for the distinction of being "a powerful indictment against anti-Semitism and other isms."

In 1948, Columbia Pictures selected Robert Young to star with Marguerite Chapman in a typical Western film, *Relentless*. Framed for a murder he didn't commit, Nick Buckley (Young) must stay one step ahead of the posse as he hunts for the man he knows to be the real killer. A fun ride for cowboy fans, but a decidedly B picture. Akin Tamiroff and Barton MacLane have supporting roles.

Nick's romantic interest, Luella Purdy, is played by Marguerite Chapman. She is prominently featured in lobby posters in a pose reminiscent of Jane Russell in *The Outlaw*. The latter film evoked much controversy over Russell's bosomy and provocative pose in its lobby posters and print ads. In Chapman's *Relentless* posters, Robert Young's face is easily overlooked in the background.

In *Sitting Pretty* (20th Century-Fox), Clifton Webb has the role of a lifetime as Lynn Belvedere, a writer secretly researching a book about the community where Harry and Tacey King reside. Robert Young and Maureen O'Hara basically provide the stage background for him as Harry and Tacey King, who are having trouble retaining a nanny for their three rambunctious boys. The name Lynn misleads them when Belvedere answers their want ad and they invite him to the house. Initially inclined to reject him, they decide to give him a try when he calmly dumps a bowl of cold oatmeal on the head of the couple's most contentious offspring.

Belvedere proves to be a dapper gentleman with many skills, a self-styled genius on everything, and of course he wins over the boys and gets them settled down. This is one of few films Webb made where he dances. Before 1944, he was an accomplished Broadway star, known for his dancing, singing, and comedic talents. Webb was so perfect as Mr. Belvedere that he repeated the role in two sequels, and played variations of the character in such films as *Cheaper by the Dozen* and *Mr. Scoutmaster*.

Ed Begley has a supporting role and Isabel Randolph appears briefly as Mrs. R. B. Frisbee, albeit unaccredited. She was undoubtedly recognized by her voice, however. A versatile radio actress, she was a frequent visitor to the folks at 79 Wistful Vista on *Fibber McGee and Molly*. She played the snooty society matron Mrs. Abigail Uppington, whom McGee nicknamed Uppy. Gentle Molly patiently endured her pretentious ramblings, but McGee was prone to aiming comic put-downs at her, which always went over her head. McGee once told Molly that Uppy had to use a longette because her nose was so out of joint that she could not wear poor folks' glasses. Randolph's character was so popular that she remained on the program for seven years.

In 1949's *Adventure in Baltimore* (RKO Radio Pictures), Robert again appears with Shirley Temple, now a lovely young women, and her off-screen husband, John Agar. In a period that predates the women's liberation movement, Dinah Sheldon (Temple) is a student at an exclusive girls' school who is raising eyebrows and blood pressures as she campaigns for women's rights. Her father, Pastor Andrew Sheldon (Young), does not approve, nor does her boyfriend Tom Wade (Agar). But she's a persuasive gal. Tom decides that he loves her too much to hold her back, and her father preaches an impromptu sermon on tolerance.

Borrowed from David O. Selznick's company, this was the second of two films that Temple and Agar did together. They were divorced soon after.

Robert next joined an all-star cast including Greer Garson, Errol Flynn, Walter Pidgeon, and Janet Leigh for MGM's *That Forsyte Woman*. It was an adaptation of the 1906 novel *The Man of Property*, by John Galsworthy, the first book in his series known as *The Forsyte Saga*. The entire series was adapted for television under the latter name as an early presentation of public television's *Masterpiece Theatre*.

The story focuses on Soames Forsyte (Flynn), a man preoccupied with material things, who treats his wife Irene (Garson) as a possession. Feeling unloved, Irene has an affair with architect Philip Bosinney (Young), but it cannot last because he is engaged to June Forsyte (Leigh), a close friend of Irene. (Are you with us so far?)

Before having to choose between the two women, Philip has an accident and dies. Irene then takes refuge with Jolyon Forsyte (Pidgeon), June's estranged father — and, yes, Jolyon is a man's name, albeit very British. A marriage seems likely, but Soames attempts a reconciliation. Will Irene consent? To be continued…

Whoops! No, that's only on *Masterpiece Theatre.*

Robert next teamed with Claudette Colbert and George Brent at RKO Radio Pictures for *Bride for Sale.* Tax expert Nora Shelley (Colbert) decides to find the perfect husband by screening through the tax records of various eligible males. Her boss, Paul Martin (Brent), gets wind of her idea and tries to teach her a lesson. He persuades his wealthy friend Steve Adams (Young) to woo and win Nora, then leave her flat. As devotees of romantic comedy would anticipate, the plan goes awry when both men find themselves falling in love with Colbert—eh, Nora—and who could resist?

The film's box office take proved to be helpful in paying RKO's taxes that year.

Columbia Pictures' *And Baby Makes Three* was a romantic comedy starring Robert Young and Barbara Hale. Jacqueline "Jackie" Walsh (Hale) has recently been divorced from Vernon Walsh (Young). Not one to dwell on past mistakes, she has found the right man for her this time in Herbert Fletcher (Robert Hutton). As she walks down the aisle, she faints, and ends up in hospital. Seems she's pregnant with Vernon's child. Can she go through with the wedding or must she return to Vernon for their child's sake?

Although done in a light-hearted style, this may have been less a comedy than a woman's handkerchief-twisting romance. Given its modest cast, it probably was a low-budget film for Columbia. Billie Burke and Herb Vigran have supporting roles, Vigran uncredited.

Elizabeth Henderson and Robert Young as they appeared in their high school yearbook. She chose to be listed as Betty. Her profile says, in part: Pres. Sr. Girls' Glee; Secy. Playcrafters; Lead in "Briar Rose" and "Sherwood"; Dept. Hon. in Music and Dramatics; Service Honors; *Lincoln High School Alumni Association*

In the 1920s, few schools had female cheer leaders. Like most, Lincoln High had a male "Yell Team." Robert Young was on the team. That's him at lower left. *Lincoln High School Alumni Association*

A postcard photo of Robert and Betty Young's alma mater; *Lincoln High School Alumni Association*

A Playcrafters' presentation of *The Taming of the Shrew*. That's Robert in the middle with the dark moustache; *Lincoln High School Alumni Association*

A scene from the Playcrafters' presentation of *Sherwood*. Bob Young starred as Robin Hood. Yearbook does not identify players, but we believe that's Bob on the right; *Lincoln High School Alumni Association*

In a play titled *East Lynn*, Robert Young, at right, gets to play the villain. (Robert Young, *a villain?*). *Pasadena Playhouse collection*

The Pasadena Playhouse, where Robert performed while enrolled in the school of theatre arts; *Pasadena Playhouse collection*

An interior view of one of the Pasadena Playhouse theaters; *Pasadena Playhouse collection*

Lt. Robert Young and wife Betty dine out at a Hollywood party. Robert was a member of the California State Guard., a branch of the state's National Guard. They were sometimes called out when a state of emergency was declared. *Associated Press photo, June, 1942*

Robert Young's womenfolk make a fuss over him in this Father's Day 1949 photo; *AP photo/Frank Filan*

Robert Young demonstrates how he keeps his girls in line in this 1954 photo. Behind Robert, from left, Carol, Barbara, Betty, and Kathy. *Associated Press photo*

Robert and Elizabeth Young pose outside the home that they nicknamed The Enchanted Cottage; *Library of Congress, LOOK magazine collection*

As he prepares to take off from Santa Monica's Clover Field, pilot Robert Young waves from his Beachcraft Bonanza plane; *Associated Press photo*

The *Father Knows Best* cast gathers around Billy Gray on cycle; from left, Robert Young, Elinor Donahue, Jane Wyatt, Lauren Chapin; *Billy Gray collection*

No crash helmet and we can't see if there's an eagle on the back of his jacket, but cyclist Robert Young is ready to hit the highway; *Billy Gray collection*

The *Father Knows Best* radio cast in a homey pose. From left in front, Rhoda Williams, Norma Jean Nillson, Ted Donaldson. Behind them, Robert Young and June Whitley; *Photofest*

Father Knows Best TV cast. Behind Lauren Chapin, from left, Billy Gray. Jane Wyatt, Robert Young, Elinor Donahue; *Billy Gray collection*

It takes a village to produce a TV series. Cast and crew of *Father Knows Best* assemble for a group photo. Dodgers' center fielder Duke Snyder, making a cameo appearance, joins them (where else?) in the center; *Lauren Chapin collection*

In a scene from *Father Knows Best*, Jim Anderson (Robert Young) has a father-daughter chat with Betty (Elinor Donahue); *Elinor Donahue collection*

Taking a break on the set, Assistant Director Herb Walerstein and Jane Wyatt turn the rope for Lauren Chapin and Robert Young. A wardrobe lady named Ena watches. If you can make out another pair of legs behind Lauren, they belong to Luz, her stand-in, waiting her turn with Robert; *Lauren Chapin collection*

In a scene from *Father Knows Best*, Betty (standing) and Margaret look on as Father reads a bedtime story to Kathy; *Elinor Donahue collection*

Lauren Chapin gets a hug from the man that she liked to call "Daddy"; *Lauren Chapin collection*

Robert Young explains to Lauren Chapin the workings of a film projector; *Lauren Chapin collection*

At one time, radio and television stations placed promos of popular programs in the entertainment section of local newspapers. These two ads promote *Father Knows Best* on both media. *Stephen Cox collection*

Father offers some supervisory advice in a *Father Knows Best* dinner scene; *Elinor Donahue collection*

Billy Gray in his motorcycle racing days and in a more recent photo; *Billy Gray collection*

Lauren Chapin and Elinor Donahue spent a day signing autographs at a nostalgia event in 2017 called The Hollywood Show; *Elinor Donahue collection*

Robert considers taking a ride on Billy's cycle, *Billy Gray collection*

Scene from *The Toy Wife*. From left, Melvyn Douglas, Luise Rainer, Robert Young; *Stephen Cox collection*

Elinor Donahue at the piano entertains Lauren Chapin and Robert Young between sets; *Elinor Donahue collection*

Promo photo of *Mortal Storm* stars. From left, Irene Rich, James Stewart, Robert Young, Frank Morgan, Margaret Sullavan; *Stephen Cox collection*

Billy Gray and Elinor Donahue in a FKB scene as Betty helps Bud get ready for a date; *Eleanor Donahue collection*

A lesson in planning ahead in a FKB scene; *Eleanor Donahue collection*

Robert enjoys the attention of FKB cast; clockwise from lower left, Billy Gray, Elinor Donahue, Jane Wyatt, Lauren Chapin; *Elinor Donahue collection*

FKB Cast surrounds Robert; clockwise from lower left, Lauren Chapin, Jane Wyatt, Billy Gray, Elinor Donahue; *Stephen Cox collection*

A *Father Knows Best* dinner scene; *Billy Gray collection*

The *Father Knows Best* TV cast takes a stroll around the studio lot. Behind Lauren Chapin, from left, Robert Young, Billy Gray, Elinor Donahue, Jane Wyatt; *Drina Mohacsi collection*

Party Time: The Hazard of Hollywood

Hollywood has long been known as a town of parties, and it was especially so in the era of the big film studios. While that is not an excuse, it may explain in part the fact that many big name stars were known for their over-indulgence, while others managed somehow to keep their drinking problems relatively hushed except among the Hollywood crowd.

Comedian W. C. Fields once said that he stopped drinking water when he saw what fish did in it. Having been born above a bar, he developed a taste for the devil's brew early on. He had a hidden stash of hundreds of bottles during prohibition, and never let it diminish after.

When filming, Fields carried a flask of gin martinis that he referred to as his "lemonade." One day a prankster on the set filled it with real lemonade. One swallow prompted a furious Fields to demand, "Who put lemonade in my lemonade?"

Fields' drinking became a source of comic material. Appearing on the Edgar Bergen and Charlie McCarthy radio program, Fields was introduced and then had this exchange with Edgar's wooden pal.

Fields: Well, if it isn't Charlie McCarthy, the woodpeckers' pin-up boy!

Charlie: Well, if it isn't W. C. Fields, the fellow who keeps Seagram's in business!

Unfortunately, there was little humor in the role that alcohol played in the lives of many in the film world. Spencer Tracy was known to be an often unruly drinker when MGM took him on. The studio retained a team known as "The Tracy Squad" to look out for him. Bars within twenty-five miles were given a number to call that would summon the team with a doctor and an ambulance.

The renowned John Barrymore took to drink even before he took to the stage in the early 1900s. By 1920, he was hailed as one of the theater's greatest talents, both for his speaking voice and his skill at encompassing his stage character. That voice made him an instant star when he switched to films in the "talkie" era, but his new friends in Hollywood included director Raoul Walsh, Anthony Quinn, and Fields. Their wild parties and antics with women got him blacklisted by most major studios in the 1930s. He died of pneumonia and cirrhosis of the liver in 1942.

Barrymore's sister Ethel also fell victim to the "family curse." She began her career in the 1890s and was soon one of the stage's brightest stars. She would become known as "The First Lady of the American Theatre" with a career that spanned six decades. But troubles in her personal life led her to begin taking refuge in drink. Fortunately, she was able to get her life back under control and became a teetotaler in her thirties. She outlived brothers John and Lionel and worked into the 1950s.

Tallulah Bankhead, Humphrey Bogart, Montgomery Clift, Errol Flynn, Robert Mitchum, and Orson Welles are but a few of the renowned stars who fell victim to the lure of alcohol. Some were known to the general public because their excesses could scarcely be kept hidden, but they mostly were forgiven while their films continued to entertain. Others were less flamboyant and avoided being written up in newspaper stories and gossip columns. Still others were able to keep their problem hidden from all but those who were closest to them.

Robert Young was one of the latter. How it came about, he scarcely even realized at the time. At some point around the time that he was diagnosed with depression, he began using alcohol to assist his prescribed medication in keeping it under control.

Robert and Elizabeth were not frequent partygoers. They were by nature homebodies. In the profession that Robert had chosen, they were occasionally obliged to attend various social gatherings. These involved some social drinking, but the Youngs would be among those who departed earliest.

Bob and Betty did not throw parties at home, but they did enjoy having friends, usually couples, for dinner and an evening together on weekends. Lucille Ball and Desi Arnaz often joined them for an evening of low-stakes poker. Lucy said that she suspected that the guys sometimes let the girls win, but if that was true it was okay with her.

The Youngs' drinking at Hollywood social gatherings was usually restrained. At home it was at first moderate, intended to be relaxing. But as Bob's depression persisted and medication brought little relief, he began to consume more alcohol to assist the drugs. On his worst days, when migraine headaches added to his woes, he sometimes locked himself in a bedroom, threw himself on the bed, and wept until he drifted off into what could not have been a very restful sleep.

Betty was a bulwark of comfort and support in his darkest hours, but she was not without her own difficulties. She, too, suffered from depression, although nothing anywhere as severe as Bob's. And because she accompanied him in his drinking, she also came to have a problem with alcohol, albeit again less severe. Even when she herself was suffering, she was there beside Bob to give him what comfort she could.

Over time, the couple's consumption increased and, for Robert, became a problem that complicated rather than eased his depression.

ON THE SCREEN AND ON THE AIR

As the 1950s approached, Robert Young wrestled with his prospects as he envisioned his acting days in a decline. He was able to discuss his concerns openly with producer Eugene B. Rodney, a long-time friend.

The two men had frequent leisurely get-togethers in which they discussed whatever was going on in their lives and around them. This often involved talk about their home lives, as both were very much family-oriented. Robert had his four daughters and Eugene had two sons. Almost always they would have some story that involved their children or the whole family. It occurred to them that, with his radio experience, Robert might play the father in a family comedy series.

The idea resulted in the creation of a partnership that they dubbed Rodney-Young Productions. Another friend, writer Ed James, was recruited to create the family situation and several scripts that would facilitate selling the idea to one of the networks. Bob's one stipulation to Ed was that he wanted to be portrayed as reasonably normal. "I'd like to be a father," he said, "but not a boob."

Radio already had its share of the latter. Dagwood Bumstead was as goofy on the *Blondie* radio series as he was in the comic strip and several films. On the *Phil Harris and Alice Faye Show*, Phil was forever getting entangled in some wacky scheme at the urging of his pal Frankie Remley. On *The Adventures of Ozzie and Harriett*, Ozzie Nelson was prone to foot-in-mouth disease and often needed to be rescued by his wife Harriett. On *The Life of Riley*, Chester A. Riley (alias William Bendix) could be counted on to say or do something each week that would put him behind the eight ball. His classic line, uttered almost every episode, was: "What a revoltin' development this is!"

Ed James soon had several completed scripts involving a family named Henderson (an insiders' tip of the hat to Bob's wife Betty), who the threesome deemed an "average American family." They were reasonably normal, albeit with some personality quirks to afford comic situations. It was a departure from the norm right off, in that the family included three children rather than the two on most other family sitcoms. Young and Rodney assembled a group of actors and an audition tape was recorded December 20, 1948. NBC execs listened and liked it, and an agreement was reached to carry a series featuring the Hendersons if a sponsor could be found. The timing was propitious.

The General Foods Company was looking for a less costly program to replace its *Maxwell House Coffee Time* program starring George Burns and Gracie Allen. They liked the Hendersons program and its price tag. In the last program of the Burns and Allen show's 1948-1949 season, Robert Young was a guest of George and Gracie as a means of introducing him and the replacement program that was coming in the Fall.

The Young, Rodney, and James trio was elated, but James had little time to celebrate. His was now the chore of writing at a robust pace so that the program would be scripted weeks, or better, months in advance. One joint decision made early on was to change the family name to Anderson, presumably because it was a more common name than Henderson.

Young and Rodney had conferred with and auditioned dozens of actors with a wide range of experience on many radio programs. Sooner than they had hoped, they had a cast. The Anderson family would be headed by Jim (Young), an insurance agent for General Insurance Company in an average Midwest town identified as Springfield, but without specifying which state. His wife, Margaret, was a stay-at-home housewife and homemaker, who often doubled as the cool-headed solver of family problems. Margaret was played in early broadcasts by June Whitley. Daughter Betty, about eighteen, son Jim Jr. (a.k.a. "Bud") about sixteen, and Kathy, eight, would be played by Rhoda Williams, Ted Donaldson, and Norma Jean Nilsson respectively. Herb Vigran, Eleanor Audley, and Sam Edwards would appear frequently as neighbors Hector and Elizabeth Smith and son Billy.

Interestingly, the Anderson children all were played by actual juveniles. Radio enabled actors with the ability to modify their voices to play all sorts of roles. Raising her voice an octave and getting whiny enabled Fanny Brice to come across as the bothersome but amusing brat, Baby Snooks. Richard Crenna had perfected the not-yet-changed voice of a teenager. He played one as a student at Madison High School on the Eve Arden series *Our Miss Brooks* and as boyfriend Oogie Pringle on *A Date with Judy*. Probably with an eye to potential publicity photographs, Young and Rodney chose to use actual youngsters.

The premiere broadcast aired August 25, 1949, originating from Los Angeles station KFI, complete with a full orchestra conducted by Roy Bargy. Bill Forman served as announcer. The show was no longer introduced as *Maxwell House Coffee Time*. Instead the series was given a title that hinted at the role Young would play, *Father Knows Best*.

When George Burns and Gracie Allen were working for General Foods, they opened their program with a little vignette before the show's actual introduction.

Gracie: Another cup of Maxwell House Coffee, George?

George: Thank you, Gracie. You know, Maxwell House is always good to the last drop.

Gracie: And that drop's good, too.

Father Knows Best likewise gave the sponsor a similar bonus plug with a brief mother-daughter exchange.

Kathy: Mother, is Maxwell House Coffee really the best-tasting coffee in the whole world?

Margaret: Well, your father says so, and your father knows best.

The premiere episode was one that may have been intended to hook fathers in the listening audience. Daughter Betty announces that she wants to marry her boyfriend, Bill Smith. Jim Anderson reacts as would many fathers in that era, dumbfounded and opposed. This is his daughter, after all. She's still just a child!

In subsequent episodes, plots aimed at presenting situations similar to what might occur in any "typical American family," if there indeed was such a thing. Robert Young and Eugene Rodney spent many hours sharing stories of goings-on in their own households and passing on to Ed James any that seemed like material for a script.

In an episode on December 29, 1949, some New Year's Eve events put Jim in a mood that makes it difficult to celebrate, much less keep his temper in check. On January 5, 1950, Bud has a problem that involves traffic court, while Jim does his best to be excused from having to make a speech about highway safety. The following week finds Jim facing a dilemma undoubtedly shared by many heads of households: the Christmas bills begin to trickle in.

The program got off to a good start, earning a favorable rating even if it did not top the charts. The Parents League of America named Robert "Outstanding Father of 1949." Listener response indicated that they accepted the Anderson family, even if they had one more child than the "average" family.

Robert spent much of his time helping to develop ideas for the program, in addition to rehearsing and performing. But he also continued to make himself available for films. It was perhaps advantageous to the radio program that 1950 brought just one opportunity.

Promoted as a mystery-suspense film, United Artists' *The Second Woman* featured Robert Young, Betsy Drake and Shirley Ballard in a rather convoluted plot. Vivian Sheppard (Ballard), fiancée of Jeff Cohalan (Young) is killed in a mysterious car accident. Cohalan's life then seems to be coming apart as his horse is injured and must be put down and his dog dies, apparently of poisoning. He begins to seclude himself in the house that he had built for Vivian, but Ellen Foster (Drake), a neighbor's niece, takes an interest in him and suspects his misfortunes are not just bad luck.

Film critic Dennis Schwartz wrote: "Robert Young gives a subdued performance that is credible, but not all that endearing." Craig Butler gave the film his lukewarm approval, writing: "*The Second Woman* is an intriguing if frustrating little thriller [that] verges on being very good but settles for being merely OK. [It] combines elements of various styles—film noir, mystery, psychological drama, thriller, romance—but doesn't meld them into a satisfying whole. All in all, a good attempt that is worth watching, even if it falls short of reaching its goals."

Based on a play of the same name, 1951's *Goodbye, My Fancy* (Warner Bros.) teamed Robert with Joan Crawford and Frank Lovejoy. Another pre-women's liberation film, it has Crawford as Congresswoman Agatha Reed returning to the college where twenty years ago she was expelled for keeping late hours. Now she is to receive an honorary degree, but what really draws her back is a lingering crush on Dr. James Merrill (Young), formerly a professor and now the college president. Eve Arden tags along as Reed's secretary, Miss "Woody" Woods. To muddy the waters, photographer Matt Cole (Lovejoy), has a crush on the congresswoman and is on hand hoping to divert her from Dr. Merrill.

Movie buffs will perhaps best remember Frank Lovejoy for appearing in the film noir *The Hitch-Hiker*. Old-time radio fans heard him on many programs and will recall him starring in the series *Night Beat* and later as John Malone on *The Amazing Mr. Malone.*

Robert did another rare Western in 1952, starring with Jack Buetel and Barton MacLane in RKO Pictures' *The Half-Breed.* It's rumored that there is a fortune in gold under land on the Arizona Apache reservation. The corrupt Marshall Cassidy (MacLane) plots to move the tribe off their land. Charlie Wolf (Buetel), known as the half-breed because of his partial European ancestry, is determined to prevent it. Gambler Dan Craig (Young) gets involved negotiating with Wolf when the townsfolk fear an Apache attack.

Jay Silverheels has an uncredited role as one of the Apaches. Born on Canada's Six Nations Reserve, he was a star lacrosse player and a boxer before becoming a movie stuntman in 1938. In a 1949 B picture called *The Cowboy and the Indians*, he worked with actor Clayton Moore. That resulted in him being chosen to star as Tonto, faithful Indian companion of the masked rider of the plains, in the *Lone Ranger* television series. Silverheels and Moore subsequently appeared together in two big-screen color films, *The Lone Ranger* (1956) and *The Lone Ranger and the Lost City of Gold* (1958).

Robert Young's big-screen career was winding down. He starred in only a handful of films during the 1950s, most of them of little note. His focus increasingly was on the *Father Knows Best* radio series, which persisted in drawing a faithful audience. Although its listener ratings were modest, it amassed its highest rating in the 1950-1951 season, a respectable 13.4. During 1951, the program was carried over thirty-nine stations of Canada's Dominion Network.

General Foods was pleased enough to continue its Maxwell House Coffee sponsorship through 1951. For some reason, it chose not renew in January, 1952, and sponsorship was taken over by the Crosley Division of Cincinnati's Avco Manufacturing. However, they did not choose to renew after the initial thirteen-week contract, and General Foods stepped in to resume sponsorship.

During the first couple of seasons, Robert was uncomfortable with the way his character came across. He got his wish not to be a boob, but he was far from the ideal head of household. Jim Anderson was at times absent-minded. He was not immune from occasionally putting his foot in his mouth, and he was at times impatient with his children. On one occasion, he even was heard to lament that he and Margaret had parented a bunch of stupid kids. Radio historian John Dunning remarks that it sometimes seemed that writer Ed James was playing the show's title for laughs.

Whether Robert raised objections, or James simply chose to move on, the writing was taken over in 1951 by Paul West. West drew upon observations of his own family as well as his children's friends and their families. Young and Rodney continued to offer occasional suggestions. As radio historian Jim Cox expressed it, West "desquabbled" the family atmosphere, and he set the tone for the program that would carry forward into its television evolution.

Young liked the result. While subsequent episodes might find Jim Anderson frustrated by a given situation, his character ultimately became a wise, easygoing father whose primary focus was the well-being of his family. He took to calling his brood by nicknames. Betty became "Princess," James Jr. was "Bud," and Kathy was either "Kitten" or "Angel." To her big brother, however, Kathy usually was "Squirt."

Margaret was still the devoted housewife who honored her husband's role as head of the house. Yet she often provided an insight that resolved the problem at hand. At times, she also took charge, as when she decreed that everyone would defer all other plans so as to facilitate a very special Father's Day.

The Anderson children's personalities contributed to various confused and amusing family situations. Betty was a bit boy crazy and had dating problems. Any little difficulty she encountered became "the worst thing that could ever happen." Bud had a steady income from a paper route, yet he always seemed to be a bit short of funds. Adolescent exasperation was apt to be expressed with his catch phrase: "Ho-ly cow!" Little sister Kathy often felt that she was overlooked. She could stir up a storm over a misplaced pair of skates, and when teasing by her siblings got to be too much, she would retort: "Awww, turn blue!"

During the years of the program's radio run, several of the original players moved on and were replaced by other seasoned performers. June Whitley (Margaret Anderson) left at the end of the second season and was replaced by film actress Dorothy Lovett. She in turn was replaced by Jean Vander Pyl during the fourth season. Norma Jean Nilsson, who by then was fourteen years old, left her role as Kathy Anderson shortly after the start of the fourth season. She was replaced by nine-year-old Helen Strohm. Mary Lee Robb, a regular on *The Great Gildersleeve*, sometimes filled in for Rhoda Williams as Betty Anderson. She later began to appear as neighbor Janey Ligget on a regular basis.

Live broadcasts of drama, comedy, and musical programs became almost a thing of the past after Bing Crosby convinced sponsor and network that a taped program not only could be of high quality reproduction but would enable the deletion of bloopers. During the 1952-1953 season, *Father Knows Best* became a taped presentation. This allowed more free time for both cast and crew to take on other projects.

That and his reduced film work afforded Robert some small degree of escape from the depression that neither drugs nor alcohol could eliminate. To add to his distress, he had begun to suffer from severe migraine headaches.

No doubt influenced to some degree by the disappearance of his father when he was a boy, Bob was very much a family man. The highlight of his week was Friday evening, when he was free to go home to his wife and daughters. He had begun to bring home films for the family to watch together. He was amused and uplifted by daughter Betty, then about eight years old, asking if he was in it. If he said he was not, she would make a show of fussing and crying, "Oh, no? Wonderful!"

Outnumbered by his womenfolk, he once told an interviewer, "It's interesting how these dames work. They appear to be on my side. They'll all agree with me. But a thing always works out the way they want. I'm not quite aware of it until it has taken place."

On another occasion, he mused that his status at home was similar to that of Jim Anderson, who *thinks* he knows best. "Every once in awhile," he admitted, "I realize that I'm being led along, gently and subtly, by the nose." His smile confirmed that he was a willing dupe.

One of Robert's last films, 1954's *The Big Moment,* was a departure from the norm. It starred John Derek, Thomas Mitchell, Donna Reed, Forrest Tucker, and Lawrence Dobkin, and was actually three short stories for which Young was designated narrator.

The first segment was the story of a homeless orphan in Casablanca who has become a thief to survive. A kind-hearted shopkeeper catches him and takes him to a United Jewish center where he is fed, clothed, and steered into an apprenticeship that will enable him to become an honest craftsman. In the second story, an immigrant doctor comes to the United States, and the third involves a girl who survived the Holocaust.

Wearing a suit and tie and speaking in what looks like a home library room or study, Young gives a short introduction to the first segment. After, he reappears to speak briefly about how the United Jewish organization seeks to help those in desperate situations, and then repeats the process for stories two and three. The film has dubbed-in Jewish speaking voices and English subtitles. Not meant for general theater distribution, it was produced by Paramount Pictures for the United Jewish Appeal. It was used as part of a fund-raising appeal and was quite effective.

Later that year, Robert appeared with Charlton Heston, Thomas Mitchell, and Nicole Maurey in the Paramount film *Secret of the Incas.* Heston is adventurer Harry Steele, on the trail of an ancient Incan artifact in Peru. His dubious associate Ed Morgan (Mitchell) wants the treasure for himself and schemes to have Harry killed. For the requisite love interest, Harry picks up Romanian defector Elena Antonescu (Maurey), who hopes to get to America. Harry's quest leads them to an archaeological dig headed by Dr. Stanley Moorehead (Young), who is preparing to enter a tomb where the jeweled ritual mask known as the Sunburst is believed to be hidden.

Film buffs often cite this film as a direct inspiration for the Indiana Jones series, with many scenes reminiscent in tone and structure to scenes in *Raiders of the Lost Ark*. Throughout most of the film, Harry Steele wears the Indiana Jones attire: brown leather jacket, fedora, tan pants, an over-the-shoulder bag, and a holstered revolver.

———

Meanwhile, things at the Anderson house continued to involve various mishaps and misunderstandings that were resolved in the last few minutes of each episode. The family plans a surprise birthday party for Jim, but his boss has an unexpected job for him. On a July end-of-season program, a family vacation is discussed and there are five different proposals. One episode is taken up with preparations for a family picnic. The circus comes to town and Kathy is dying to go, but no one is keen on taking her. A Halloween story has the family car running out of gas next to a cemetery on a dark night.

On one program, Jim lectures his family on doing more than is expected of you and is then asked to chaperone a sleigh ride planned by Betty's friend. A day spent cleaning out the attic presents a series of surprises. But when the basement needs to be cleaned out, Jim finds that he must make an important business trip. In an episode that would seem silly today, the delivery of an automatic washing machine is a big event. Trying to make an impression on a boy she likes, Betty pretends to be a Southern belle. On another occasion, Jim bets his daughter the price of a new dress that she can't stop mentioning or talking to boys for twenty-four hours. And then there was the time that he came home to find his wife modeling a $3,000 mink coat! She only has it on approval, but she does look just divine in it.

Sponsors varied during the program's five-year run. General Foods chose to promote its Maxwell House Coffee during the first two years. It later began mixing in commercials for other products such as Postum (breakfast cereal), Post Wheat Meal, and Post 40% Bran Flakes. It even bumped Maxwell House in favor of hawking Sanka, its instant coffee. During Crosley's tenure, the company touted various appliances. The program was popular enough that NBC carried it on a sustaining (unsponsored) basis for a time between sponsors and near the end of its run.

When General Foods switched from Maxwell House Coffee commercials to touting its various breakfast cereals, the program did a variation of its opening mini-introduction.

Kathy: Mother, are 40 Percent Bran Flakes really the best-tasting cereal of them all?

Margaret: Well, your father says so, and your father knows best.

In 1950, noting that one third of all teenage deaths were due to car accidents, President Truman's Highway Safety Committee in Washington, D.C., recruited Bob to spearhead its safety campaign for young drivers. As part of a massive campaign to educate teen drivers, those who signed up to join the Robert Young Good Drivers' Club received a booklet with his picture on the cover. As a real-life father, Bob felt strongly about supporting the campaign. It was mentioned as a public service at the end of each week's program.

Father Knows Best never ranked among radio's highest rated programs, but in 1950 it achieved a respectable rating of 13.4. On the three networks' Thursday night schedules, it began in a modest ninth place. However, as its popularity grew, it advanced to fourth, second, and finally first place in the 1952-1953 season with a score of 28 points.

During 1954, *Father Knows Best*, along with many other radio programs, suffered a dwindling audience. Not because of any decline in program quality, but due to the lure of a new medium that Newton Minow called the "vast wasteland." Even with its small flickering screens, poor reception, and mostly mediocre programming, more and more Americans were being drawn away from radio by the novelty of television.

Nevertheless, NBC deemed *Father Knows Best* a quality program worth carrying through its last season on a sustaining basis. The last radio episode aired on April 25, 1954.

———

FROM SILVER SCREEN TO SMALL SCREEN

Given his many years working in films, it's not surprising that Robert Young explained he had felt himself "drawn to television like a man in a canoe heading for Niagara Falls." Keenly aware of radio's faltering status as family entertainment, he and Eugene Rodney began planning ahead for a transition. As early as mid-1952, an announcement went out that *Father Knows Best* would be adapted to television.

Early in 1953, in partnership with Screen Gems, Young-Rodney Productions began making preparations for a filmed pilot program. Since a positive audience response could not be assured, it would not be called *Father Knows Best*. Instead it would be presented as a one-time family comedy-drama titled "Keep It In the Family." It would, nevertheless, star Robert Young as the head of an identical family of five.

Robert was Jim Warren. His wife Grace was played by Ellen Drew. The children were older daughter Peggy, son Jeff, and younger daughter Patty, played by Sally Fraser, Gordon Gebert, and Tina Thompson. The story has Peggy dreaming of becoming a famous actress after she is discovered by a talent scout. Unfortunately, the "scout" is a fellow looking for hopefuls to attend his acting school.

"Keep It in the Family" aired as a presentation of *Ford Theatre* on May 27, 1954. Response was sufficiently positive that Young and Rodney determined to proceed. They would need a studio for filming, for they had already decided that the show would not be done live. Many of television's early programs were live, and they were prone to even more bloopers than on radio. Remember

Betty Furness and that refrigerator? Also, as Rodney observed, "There's nothing that'll grow ulcers faster than trying to do a live show with children."

The set for what would become the Anderson home was on Stage 11 at the studios of Columbia Pictures, known as Sunset Gower Studios. It was the first studio to be used exclusively for filming television programs.

Screen Gems would be filming with one camera on a closed set. Unlike most film stages, the home's rooms had four walls rather than just three. This enabled many different camera angles and gave viewers the impression that they were looking into a real house. One area sufficed for all four bedrooms by having interchangeable wallpapered walls. The set's kitchen was real. Lunches were kept in the refrigerator, and every morning coffee and sweet rolls were served to cast and crew.

Recruiting a cast was the first crucial task. Other than Robert Young, none of the cast from "Keep It in the Family" was deemed quite right for television's Anderson family. As producer, Eugene Rodney was tasked with finding just the right players. He interviewed and auditioned over two hundred hopefuls.

Lauren Chapin won the role of young Kathy. She was one of seventy-eight girls who tried out for the part. When Rodney had reduced the candidates to ten, they each did a screen test. The tests were developed, spliced together, and delivered to the Young home, where the family watched them together. At least two other girls were the right size and deemed excellent in their performances, but a decision was made when Bob observed to his family that Lauren looked very much like daughter Kathy.

Elinor Donahue, who began singing on radio at age two, was a seasoned 16-year-old actress when she auditioned twice for Rodney. The first time, he shook his head and said that she looked "too little girl." The second time, she padded her bra and wore a waist cincher. Which led Rodney to moan, "Too sophisticated."

Then her persistent agent wrangled a screen test with Robert. She was so nervous as they prepared for the test that she began to cry. The patient, fatherly Bob told her to just calm down and asked, "Would you like a Coca-Cola?" After he got it for her, she was able to do the test, but she was sure that she had blown it. A month later, she was speechless when her agent called her to say that she'd been chosen for the role.

Rodney was perhaps most frustrated trying to fill the role of James Jr., "Bud." More than thirty boys and young men auditioned for the part, and it seemed none could get the right teenaged boy's abstraction that he was looking for. Rodney wanted someone who could say gag lines — what he and Young dubbed "Budisms" — without a "this-is-a-joke, see?" lilt.

As an example, he cited a scene in which Jim, worried about Betty going steady, reads aloud a newspaper story about a girl who eloped and took $200 with which her aunt planned to buy a TV set. Bud looks up and asks seriously, "What size screen, Dad?" At last, Billy Gray auditioned, and Rodney said, "Billy was the only actor that could do it the way we wanted." Billy became James Jr.

Rodney might have been elated at finding the right people to play the Anderson siblings, but an even more important role had to be filled: Mrs. Jim Anderson, Margaret. Rodney made a list of possible candidates. Then he trimmed it down to a dozen and consulted with his partner.

Jane Wyatt was the name at the top of Rodney's list. Robert knew Wyatt and was familiar with her work. He told Eugene that he thought she would be perfect for the role. Eugene agreed, and told Bob he would get her.

Easier said than done. Rodney contacted Wyatt, told her about the proposed television series and invited her to fill the role of Margaret. She turned him down. Living in New York with her investment broker husband, Edgar Ward, and their two sons, she was a Broadway veteran who made her screen debut in 1934 and appeared in more than thirty movies. Having now made a home in New York, she was still quite active, appearing on numerous television programs and occasional stage performances when the opportunity arose. The prospect of commuting to California didn't appeal to her, and as she told an interviewer in 1990, "I'd been doing a lot of live TV drama in which I was the star. I didn't want to be just a mother."

When all of his persuasive appeal did not change her mind, Rodney sent her a copy of the first episode's script with a sincerely worded note asking her to reconsider. It lay on a table for more than a month until Edgar encouraged Jane to at least give it a read. She did, and she loved it. She later recalled, "It changed my life." She called Rodney to tell him she was on board.

Father Knows Best TV cast, clockwise from top: Robert Young, Jane Wyatt, Elinor Donahue, Billy Gray, Lauren Chapin; *Nostalgia Digest Collection*

As a cast was being assembled, scripts were being prepared by Paul West, who was joined by fellow writer Roswell Rogers. Rogers' family included three children and the West family had four. They drew many ideas from happenings within their own families and sought to develop stories that would prompt viewers to say, "That happened to us once." Both Rodney and Young continued to make occasional suggestions, and Rodney noted that many scripts had what he called "built-in moral lessons."

William D. Russell joined the team as director. When Jane Wyatt arrived from New York, filming began. Mondays and Tuesdays were devoted to rehearsals. Actual filming took place Wednesday through Friday. If they didn't finish, they had to work Saturdays. Juvenile actors, which included Lauren Chapin and Elinor Donahue, were not allowed to work overtime.

William Russell was a big man with a big commanding voice, but he also was a man who wept easily. Robert Young recalled that the cast could gauge how well they had done on a sentimental scene by observing Russell after he called, "Cut!" If his cheeks were wet, they had done well.

Things progressed smoothly, and the television adaptation of *Father Knows Best* was ready to commence in the Fall of 1954. In spite of its long radio run on NBC, it was picked up by CBS. A lack of time slots may have been a factor. CBS scheduled it to air on Sunday evenings at 10:00 P.M. Eastern Time. Not an ideal time to attract adult viewers, it meant there probably would be no juvenile audience there and few in the Midwest time zone.

The lack of a juvenile audience was not a deterrent to the Lorillard Tobacco Company, and they signed on as sponsor to promote their filtered Kent cigarettes. With that necessity satisfied, the program made its debut on October 3, 1954.

In what became the standard opening to each episode, Jim Anderson was seen entering the house in suit and tie and calling out what became a series catchphrase: "Margaret! I'm home!" Then, in what also became a patented routine, he went to the hall closet, removed his suit coat and replaced it with a leisurely sweater. (One wonders if a young Fred Rogers was watching.)

As with its radio predecessor, the television series attempted to present realistic, if somewhat exaggerated, stories of family incidents, mix-ups, or misunderstandings. Rather than belly laughs, it strove for chuckles and perhaps heads nodding understandingly.

The first episode involved Bud inviting a girl named Marcia to a dance, even though he can't dance. Jim goes to tactfully warn Marcia and learns that she doesn't dance either. Jim ends up teaching her some steps, while Bud is learning at home from big sister Betty.

The following week, Jim lectures his brood about good citizenship. They listen and respond by taking on various community volunteer projects, which cause Father some unanticipated complications.

One episode involves the family getting a new washing machine (sound familiar?). Fascinated, Kathy can't resist throwing things into it. A few weeks later, she makes up for it by writing a Thanksgiving poem for a school assignment and having it chosen as the best. Which leads proud Father to think there is a future celebrity in the family.

The November 28 episode was one to which all parents could relate. Agreed that their kids are responsible enough to stay home and fend for themselves for a weekend, Jim and Margaret plan a second honeymoon. Then Betty gets several phone calls from a boy she does not like and tells Bud and Kathy not to answer the phone. Their parents try to call home to check on them, and when there is no answer they panic.

The show continued through its first season with such low-key difficulties and mishaps that sought not guffaws but smiles of understanding. Jim Anderson personified the husband and father to whom family always came first, and Margaret assisted him in his times of confusion as the voice of reason.

Father Knows Best paid attention to literate dialogue, and filming was done with movie-style precision. Rodney, Young, and the writers sought to present some simple message about family life in each episode without appearing to preach. As Rodney said, "Good scripts weren't big action or bagfuls of jokes. We sought character, motivation."

In its first year, *Father Knows Best* was greeted by viewers and critics with what one reviewer called "polite enthusiasm." Viewer numbers were not impressive, but many of those who stayed up late enough to watch did send letters of appreciation.

The Lorillard people were unimpressed and chose not to renew sponsorship for the next season. Unable to find another sponsor, CBS announced that the program would be dropped.

Rating numbers may not have been impressive, but the show had attracted enough regular viewers that CBS soon began receiving letters of protest. Most said something like: "This is one of the few shows that our whole family watches. We even learn something from it." Newspaper columnists got wind of this and took up the call, some with vehement articles. They began urging viewers to write directly to William Paley, president of CBS. Many pointed out that the show might have a higher rating if it was on at a more reasonable hour.

It's worth noting that, in spite of its low rating, *Father Knows Best* won the 1954 Sylvania award for "outstanding family entertainment." Sylvania Electric Products (whose products included television sets) gave out the awards between 1951 and 1959 for categories such as performance, scripts, music, and other aspects of the medium. Unlike the Emmy, which would simply decorate a mantel, the Sylvania trophy was a precision clock. A sculpture of a robed woman is mounted on a walnut wood base and carries the clock face on her shoulder. It had gilt stars at each hour and stylized lightning bolts for hands. In terms of prestige, the award rivaled that of the Emmy, but it was discontinued when Sylvania merged into GTE.

The viewer protests did not dissuade Paley and CBS from cancelling *Father Knows Best*, but people in the marketing department at Scott Paper Company took note. The company stepped forward to become the show's sponsor. One columnist noted that this was a rare instance when a program really was brought back "by popular demand."

Scott Paper moved the program to NBC, perhaps because they were more flexible or had an opening in their scheduling. Beginning in the Fall of 1955, the series began airing at 8:30 P.M. ET on Wednesdays. Ratings did indeed improve thereafter. Within a year, there were 19 million households tuned in at the new time. By 1960, *Father Knows Best* was finishing in the top ten every week!

Midway through the television run of *Father Knows Best*, a joyful event took place within the Young family. Having been married in a small, unattended ceremony performed by a justice of the peace, Robert and Elizabeth, encouraged by their four daughters, arranged to have a "real" wedding performed. It was held on March 6, 1958, their twenty-fifth anniversary, in the Episcopal chapel of the Bishop School in La Jolla, the alma mater of all the Young daughters. The ceremony was performed by the Episcopal chaplain. Robert's best man was Kenneth Morrison, the justice of the peace from their first wedding, now a Superior Court judge.

———

Spurred on by *Father Knows Best*'s popularity in its television reincarnation, the cast, crew, and writers worked diligently to keep a steady flow of shows "in the can." Most of the time, they were fifteen to seventeen episodes ahead of schedule. William Russell directed the first sixty-two episodes. When he left, the cast and crew adapted to the style of a younger, soft-spoken man named Peter Tewksbury, who directed most of the remaining 141 episodes. As a shoot was about to begin, the assistant director would shout: "Quiet!" Then Tewksbury would say pleasantly, "All right, now. HAPPY! ACTION!"

Still committed to his role as a promoter of safe teen driving, Robert suggested an episode in which Bud is made to serve as a school crossing guard after an incident in which he misuses his father's car. Copies of the film were distributed to many schools for use in their drivers' education classes. With Robert's help, the program eventually enlisted almost four million members in the Good Drivers' Club. In May, 1959, Robert flew to Toronto, donned a dinner jacket, and in solemn tones addressed the Canadian Highway Safety Conference on mass media's role in traffic safety.

Also in 1959, the U.S. Treasury Department commissioned a special 30-minute episode of the show titled "24 Hours in Tyrant Land." It was a promotion for the sale of savings bonds. Not intended to be aired on television, copies of the episode were distributed to schools, churches, and civic groups.

Other episodes with subtle messages were often requested for use in schools and by public service organizations. But Eugene Rodney insisted, "We don't try to preach or instruct. We only make an effort to entertain…in honest and believable situations." That, he believed, made *Father Knows Best* appealing to educators and service organizations. Few television shows received as many requests for prints and scripts.

The *Father* cast developed a bit of a family atmosphere, even though they did little socializing off the set. Lauren Chapin,

Elinor Donahue and Billy Gray came to have a sort of sibling relationship, talking and playing together at times, and at other times getting into mischief or teasing one another.

Director William Russell remembered a frustrating effort to get on film a scene in which the three Anderson children sat at a table doing their respective school homework. Every time Billy had a line, he blew it. After more than a dozen frustrating repeats, Russell learned that Lauren could throw Billy off by poking him under the table.

For his part, Billy discovered that, by making off-camera signals to Lauren, he could cause Elinor to flub her lines. That would cause her to burst into tears and run off the set.

Russell said, "Those kids all gave us trouble at first. There were days, driving home, when I wondered how we'd ever keep the show on the air."

Nevertheless, they did. Other than Lauren and Elinor, whose ages prohibited them from overtime, they put in as much as twelve hours a day, five days a week, forty-five weeks a year. A prevailing rule was that there must be a twelve-hour break between shoots. So, if a difficult session ran until ten or eleven o'clock in the evening, cast and crew could not be called back until ten or eleven the next day.

Lauren, who lived with her divorced mother, adopted Robert as her surrogate father. Arriving on the set in the morning, she would rush up to him, kiss him on the cheek, and say, "Hi, Daddy." Robert accepted it with a fatherly smile.

Elinor's parents also divorced when she was young. Older and more reserved than Lauren, she never could bring herself to call Robert "Daddy," or Bob, as Billy did. Instead, she always addressed him as Mr. Young. She professes that she would have complied had he said, "Oh, for heaven's sake, call me Bob!" He didn't, and she didn't. But when they were seated next to each other, she often reached over to pat his hand and got his warm smile in response.

Young may have seen Billy as the son he never had. They had some long, semi-serious conversations. Bob had a motorcycle that he mostly rode for fun on weekends. Billy owned a motorcycle, rode it to the set each day, and had a prohibitive clause put in his contract when it was learned that he was an enthusiastic cycle drag racer. He and Bob sometimes discussed the relative merits of various bikes. When Bob's MG broke down on him one day, Billy's skill with engines enabled him to get it running again.

During one of their conversations, Bob confided to Billy that when *Father Knows Best* was being transitioned to television he had stipulated that the title should end with a question mark, indicating the obvious assumption that father didn't *always* know best. The people at Kent would not hear of it, and although Bob at first considered that a deal breaker, he relented for the sake of all those who were invested in the program's television future. But although flattered when Billy occasionally asked his advice, Robert said he "would feel presumptuous in suggesting I assume the position of a father" for the young man.

For her part, Jane Wyatt acknowledged that she came to share with the group a sense that they were a sort of family while together on the lot. She recalled once being invited to dinner at the Youngs' home. When she arrived and Robert greeted her, she instinctively reached out to straighten his tie.

Wyatt also had a high regard for Eugene Rodney, despite her initial efforts to shoo him off. She told of once asking him what she could do to come across better as the mother of the Anderson children. Rodney, a devoted family man, replied, "Love your kids more."

It hit home with Jane, who realized that she had been a bit rough on her two boys recently about their school work. She resolved to begin focusing more on their praiseworthy aspects and less on their shortcomings.

Elinor remembered that almost all the adults smoked. At times the stage doors had to be opened to let the haze out for filming.

Jane Wyatt, a non-smoker, had it in her contract that they would take a break at four o'clock for her tea time. She had a large pot of tea brewed and would share it with the juvenile cast and anyone else nearby, along with a cake or cookies.

Lauren, Elinor, and Billy never knew at the time of Bob's drinking problem. Wyatt and the directors and perhaps a few others did, although he mostly managed to keep that part of his life separate from his professional life.

No doubt there were days when Robert came to work suffering the effects of a previous night's drinking. For the most part, he valiantly held himself together and got through the days. On a few rare occasions he left early. Cast and crew were told that Mr. Young was not feeling well and they were dismissed for the day.

Years later, Elinor recalled that Bob had five or six male friends who occasionally came, individually, to visit and keep him company in his trailer. When she learned of his problem, she realized they were members of his Alcoholics Anonymous group that he had called to help him get through the day. One of these men was Cliff Edwards, who provided the voice of the Walt Disney character Jiminy Cricket. One day, as he was leaving, Elinor briefly chatted with him and innocently asked why he was there. Edwards grinned at her and said that he and Bob were members of the same club.

In spite of his problems, Robert usually was able to put in the long hours, always knew his lines, and was patient, offering encouragement and suggestions to others when they had difficulties. Between sets, the three young people sometimes got frisky and began behaving like real siblings. When their teasing or horsing around got to be a bit much, it usually was Jane Wyatt who became the surrogate mother and said sternly, "All right now, you kids. That's enough."

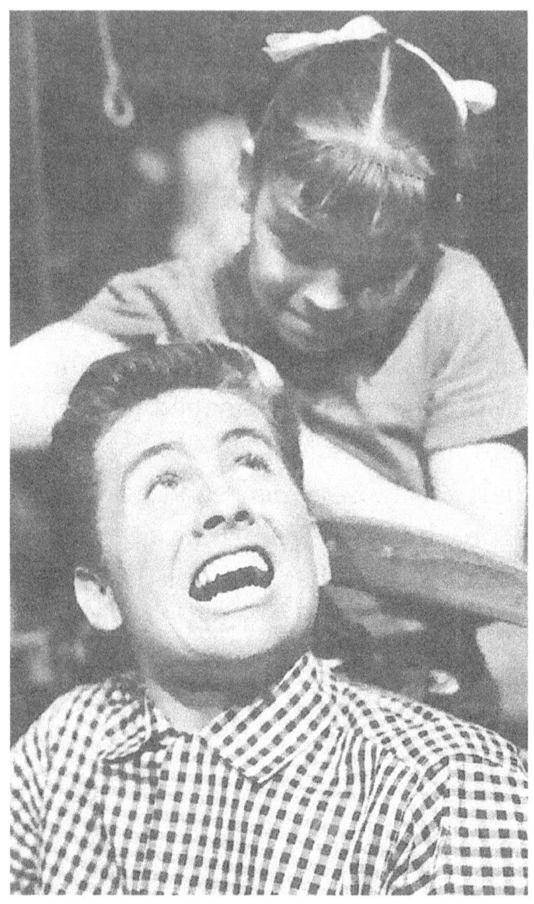

Playful Lauren pesters Billy; *Lauren Chapin collection*

On a few occasions, Jane was in her trailer and Robert was reading his newspaper when the ruckus started. He made no verbal reprimand. Instead, he merely removed his glasses, put them in his pocket, got up with the newspaper tucked under his arm, and quietly left the area. The threesome would look at one another with expressions that said, "Oh, oh. We better settle down." Then quiet would prevail…until next time.

Although Jane Wyatt was an occasional dinner guest of the Youngs, the *Father Knows Best* cast did little fraternizing off the lot. However, the three young stars developed a bond and were in touch periodically in later years.

About Robert, Jane Wyatt later recalled that, although they did little socializing off the set, "we were together every day for six years, and during that time he never pulled rank [and] always treated his on-screen family with the same affection and courtesy he showed his loved ones in his private life."

With Scott Paper still sponsoring, the program moved back to CBS in September, 1958, where it aired at 8:30 P.M. ET on Mondays. From late 1957 through 1960, Lever Brothers became an alternating sponsor.

Often criticized as portraying a too-perfect family, *Father Knows Best* did have a sort of Norman Rockwell appeal to it, with cheery if imperfect characters. The children were well-behaved and respected their parents. The parents were loving and patient with their children's faults. Someone referred to it as an airbrushed portrait of family life that ordinary folk watching could relate to and hope to emulate. One reviewer wrote early on: "Jim Anderson may be the first intelligent father permitted on TV since they invented the thing."

In addition to its Sylvania award, the program won the 1955 National Association for the Betterment of Radio and TV Award, a Christopher Award, and the 1955 Family Service TV Award. In 1956, Robert Young won the Emmy for Best Continuing Performance by an Actor in a Leading Role in a Dramatic or Comedy Series. In 1957, he won the award again, and shared the spotlight with Jane Wyatt, who won for Best Continuing Performance by an Actress in a Leading Role in a Dramatic or Comedy Series. Wyatt went on to win the award again in 1958 and 1959. Peter Tewksbury won the 1959 award for Best Director for a Single Program of a Comedy Series: "Medal for Margaret."

For the 1959 Emmy ceremony, Jane Wyatt was out of town and unable to attend. Lauren Chapin was delighted when Jane asked her to be her representative. Wearing a lovely new pink silk and lace dress, Lauren sat enthralled next to her escort,

Robert Young. She fidgeted nervously and excitedly as they sat through the long evening of awards. Her new shoes were too tight and hurt her feet, so she kicked them off. When they heard the announcement that Wyatt had won, Lauren let out a cry of joy and excitement and dashed up onto the stage, barefoot. Like a dutiful father, Robert followed her with her shoes and helped her get them back on her feet. The incident prompted a burst of laughter from the audience, followed by a round of applause. It was one of the highlights of the evening.

Robert Young, who had been continually downcast and worried about his future and his ability to provide for his family during his film years, was now the star, co-producer and co-owner of an award-winning television series that ran for six years with a faithful viewing audience.

But by 1960, Bob had grown weary of playing the near-perfect father. As scripts called for Betty to get married and Jim Jr. to join the army, he felt that the program had run the gamut. It was time to draw the curtains. He said, "We're doing a show about two adults, and three other adults, and it's getting silly." He announced that the program would not continue for another season.

A writers' strike unexpectedly shut down the studio during filming of what would have been one of the last episodes. Rodney and Young chose not to recall everyone when the strike was settled. Having reached a total of 203 television episodes, *Father Knows Best* aired its last on September 17, 1960. There was no one last gathering for a goodbye party. Elinor Donahue remembered that "I felt like a bird kicked out of the nest."

But that was not "The End." *Father Knows Best* was so popular that when production ended, it continued in primetime network reruns for the next three years. No other show had ever done that. It then ran another four years (until 1967) on ABC's daytime line-up. Through the decades of the 1970s, 1980s and 1990s, it was on both local and cable channels such as the (CBN) Family Channel. In 2000 through 2003, it aired on TVLand. As of this writing, the Antenna TV Network is broadcasting episodes on weekdays and weekends at various times. That is a remarkable testimony to the quality of the program and the performances of those who starred in it.

WHAT COMES NEXT?

Thanks to his part-ownership of *Father Knows Best*, Robert Young was now a millionaire. This at a time when a million dollars actually was a lot of money. As Senator Everett Dirksen said during a speech protesting government spending: "A million here, and a million there. Pretty soon it adds up to real money."

Asked what he would do now that the popular television series was ended, Robert said, "My immediate plans? To play more golf. My future plans are in a state of flux. I plan to take my family to Europe this summer for a vacation. Beyond that, I haven't a clue."

Bob did manage to spend some relaxing leisure time with Betty. When possible, they gathered with some or all of their girls.

But he was still plagued with depression and fierce headaches. Regular visits with his AA group were helpful, but when the pain and anxiety persisted, he sought refuse in alcohol.

Acting was in his blood, and being engaged gave him some degree of escape from his troubles. So he continued making cameo appearances on various television series, and even was a guest on *The Dick Cavett Show*.

Then he allowed a friend to talk him into what he later called a big mistake. He agreed to star in a series called *Window on Main Street*. Written by Roswell Rogers, it involved a newspaper reporter in a small town who observed people passing under his apartment window, picking out one each week, and developing a human interest story for the paper.

Bob accepted the role on condition that his partner Eugene Rodney would be the producer. Eugene may have regretted it as much as Bob did. The show did not catch on, and airing opposite *The Rifleman* and *The Price is Right*, it lasted only from October 2, 1961 to May 23, 1962. As Bob explained, the show lacked both warmth and drama. "I played the town busybody," he said, "kind of a male Mary Worth. It lasted one season, and I was delighted when it was cancelled."

Bob and Betty decided it was time to retire. Two of their daughters were grown and the others almost. They moved to Rancho Santa Fe, a resort community built around a golf course, twenty-five miles north of San Diego. They built a modest two-bedroom house and named it "the Enchanted Cottage," because it reminded them of the house Bob's character rented in the film of that name.

It worked for a while. He and Betty continued to avoid the Hollywood party scene, instead having a few friends over for dinner occasionally. Bob spent most of his time with family, but accepted a few offers to appear as a guest star on various shows. He found some release in the work. Recalling an appearance on *The Name of the Game*, in which he got to play an eccentric millionaire, he fondly remembered getting to say, "I got enough money to be able to wear white socks. You got enough money to be able to wear white socks?" His friends at General Foods also recruited him to be a spokesperson for their Sanka instant coffee, doing television commercials for five years.

Unfortunately, Robert's depression and migraine headaches were not diminished by his minimizing the pressures of performing. In 1966, he suffered what was then typically described as a nervous breakdown. He was hospitalized for exhaustion, aggravated by alcoholism.

When released, he withdrew from performing entirely. Although he and Elizabeth had not been churchgoers, he experimented with the practice of the Science of the Mind, a sort of spiritual metaphysics. Teaching that we live in a spiritual Universe, that God is in, around, and for us, the Science of the Mind stresses a willingness to let the inner Spirit guide our living. It proved somewhat comforting for Robert, but like alcohol and his medications it could not dispel his inner demon of depression and the physical pain of his migraine headaches.

—

Is There a Doctor in the House?

Early in 1969, word on the Hollywood grapevine was that the year's most certain television hit would be a projected series about a doctor whose office is in his home. Producer David Victor had tentatively lined up Ralph Bellamy to star, but he let it be known that he would like to have Robert Young. The two had worked together a few times and had a good rapport.

Word reached Robert. He was restless, and he was interested. He visited Victor in his office. They chatted a bit and David gave Robert an overview of the show's premise. Robert was intrigued by the role he would play, and he accepted. The series would be titled *Marcus Welby, M.D.* Robert returned home with the script for a stand-alone TV movie that would introduce the series and its characters.

A pilot film, "A Matter of Humanities," aired as an *ABC Movie of the Week* on March 26, 1969. Robert played an old-fashioned family practitioner, Dr. Marcus Welby, with a kindly bedside manner, who ran his own small practice from an office in his home. A young James Brolin played his associate, Dr. Steve Kiley. Elena Verdugo played Consuelo Lopez, Welby's dedicated nurse and office manager.

Born April 20, 1925, in Paso Robles, California, Elena Verdugo began taking dancing lessons while in kindergarten and made her first screen appearance when she was six. In numerous supporting roles, she appeared in thirty-one films between 1931 and 1970, often as an enticing Spanish lady or gypsy. Her vocal versatility and flair for comedy earned her guest spots on many radio programs. From 1952 to 1956, she starred on the comedy series *Meet Millie*, first on radio, then television. She also appeared in guest roles on numerous television programs. Although she did not win, she was twice nominated for an Emmy for her *Welby* role.

In the *Welby* pilot film, Lew Ayres makes a cameo appearance as Dr. Andrew Swanson of the nearby Lang Memorial Hospital. Older viewers remembered Ayres as the star of numerous *Dr. Kildare* films in the 1930s and 1940s. The 90-minute special received good reviews and viewer response, and plans moved forward swiftly to begin production of the series.

Marcus Welby, M.D. premiered on September 23, 1969. During the opening credits of each episode, viewers were reminded of the generation gap between the two doctors. Welby would be seen driving his dated sedan. Kiley would arrive at the hospital astride his motorcycle. In the initial episode, Robert's *Welby* character is established as a kindly family practitioner with a bedside manner, who is on a first-name basis with many of his patients, and also makes house calls.

Brolin's Dr. Kiley is a bit brash, headstrong, and a more progressive type, who sometimes takes issue with Welby's style or prognosis. Yet some of Welby's personal caring for their patients rubs off on him. The handsome, six foot, four inch Brolin qualified as what girls in that era often referred to as a heartthrob. (Today it probably would be a hunk.) His presence in the cast may have attracted many young female viewers who might otherwise not have watched.

In that regard, however, the program had the good fortune to be on at the same time as the *CBS News Hour*, and once every fourth week NBC aired its *First Tuesday* series. In what might have seemed an unfavorable time slot, the show soon established itself as the top-rated program in all television. As a writer in *TV Guide* observed, "Well over two-thirds of homes viewing television at 10 to 11 P.M. decided *Welby* is the least objectionable program." That might sound like a backhanded compliment, but in 1970 and 1971 the show became the first series on ABC to top the Nielsen ratings for an entire season. It went on to be one of the top fifteen shows for four seasons, from 1969 to 1973.

Marcus Welby cast, from left, Robert Young, Elena Verdugo, James Brolin; *Stephen Cox collection*

In 1970, Young won his third Emmy and Brolin his first, for Outstanding Performance by an Actor in a Supporting Role. He was subsequently nominated three more times, although he did not win. He also was nominated for Golden Globes three times for Best Supporting Actor, and won twice, in 1971 and 1973. The show itself won for Outstanding Dramatic Series, and Young won a Golden Globe in 1972 for his performance.

Starring in an on-going award-winning series did not prevent Bob from occasionally taking on another role. In 1971, he appeared in two episodes of a short-lived series called *Vanished*. Revolving around a disappearance of the president, each episode was a stand-alone story with various guest stars, including Richard Widmark, Tom Bosley, Betty White, Larry Hagman, Eleanor Parker, E.G. Marshall, William Shatner, and even Chet Huntley in a cameo appearance as a newscaster.

That same year, he starred on another series that lasted but one season. On *Robert Young and the Family*, his role actually was to act as host, introducing a weekly series of stand-alone sketches poking fun at the American family. Guest stars included Beau Bridges, Lee Grant, Dick Van Dyke, Lurene Tuttle, Jack Warden and others.

In 1972, Robert starred in a made-for-television film called *All My Darling Daughters*. The widowed father of four daughters (played by Darlene Carr, Judy Strangis, Sharon Gless, and Lara Parker) must cope with the unlikely but comical circumstances that lead to all four getting married on the same day. Viewer response was positive enough to prompt a sequel titled *My Darling Daughters' Anniversary*. This time Father is preparing to remarry. His bride-to-be is played by Ruth Hussey. Raymond Massey, renowned for his portrayal of Abraham Lincoln, played the girls' grandfather in both films.

For Robert, the father of four daughters in real life, the two films had to be a bit of a lark.

Ruth Hussey and Robert Young prepare to tie the knot on the TV special My Darling Daughters' Anniversary; *Stephen Cox collection*

With his once slick black hair taking on a silvery color, Robert Young looked very much the mature, wise physician who knew more about his long-time patients than just their illnesses. In the premiere episode, he's seen at a high school football scrimmage. When a reporter making notes asks why he isn't attending to his patients, he responds, "I delivered some of those boys. If they're good enough to finally make the city playoffs, I don't want them bent out of shape!"

Welby had known many of his patients since birth or soon after, and often could diagnose problems in short order. (He had only ninety minutes each episode, after all.) Storylines for the series covered the waterfront, including impotence, depression, brain damage, breast cancer, mononucleosis, sexually transmitted diseases, epilepsy, rape, learning disabilities, leukemia, Alzheimer's Disease, addiction to painkillers, and more.

Members of the American Academy of Family Physicians served as technical advisers for the series and reviewed every script for medical accuracy. Yet many in the medical profession took issue with the good doctor's ability to deal with all of these, or at least identify the problem and make the proper referral. But in an era when specialized medicine was becoming the norm, others credited Welby for referring patients to those who could properly treat them, and when an operation was required, Welby would be in the surgical theater observing.

There once was a burst of angry protests from the gay community when Welby advised a middle-aged man to resist his homosexual impulses. Seven sponsors refused to buy advertising time on the program, and seventeen network affiliates refused to air the episode. This was the first known instance of network affiliates refusing a network episode in response to protests. Also, an episode dealing with abortion was refused by San Diego area ABC affiliate XETV.

Even so, when the opposing news programs were moved, *Marcus Welby, M.D.* continued to be one of the four most watched series on all television. Its popularity attracted many well known stars to make guest appearances in cameo roles. Among them: Jack Albertson, Richard Basehart, Anne Baxter, Tom Bosley, Albert Brooks, Jackie Coogan, Cathy Lee Crosby, Rosemary DeCamp, Don DeFore, Howard Duff, Patty Duke, Sally Field, Chief Dan George, Virginia Gregg, Ruth Hussey, Jack Kelly, Dorothy Lamour, June Lockhart, Agnes Moorehead, Margaret O'Brien, Walter Pidgeon, Pernell Roberts, Ruth Roman, Tom Selleck, William Shatner, Craig Stevens, Robert Urich, and Chill Wills.

In an episode on March 12, 1974, titled "Designs," Robert was reunited with Jane Wyatt, his old friend and former co-star from the television series of *Father Knows Best*. She played a fashion designer whose marriage to an embittered paraplegic led her to fall in love with the doctor while keeping her marriage a secret most of the episode. June Whitley and Rhoda Williams, who played Margaret Anderson and daughter Betty respectively on the radio version of the show, each appeared several times in incidental roles.

The show also enjoyed two crossover stories with the series *Owen Marshall: Counselor at Law*. In "Men Who Care," Marshall defends the father of Welby's patient when the man is accused of murdering his daughter's boyfriend. In "I've Promised You a Father," Marshall defends Dr. Kiley in a paternity suit filed by a nurse claiming that Kiley is the father of her child.

Fortunately, Kiley is cleared and is able to marry the hospital's public relations director Janet Blake (played by Pamela Hensley) in 1975, at the beginning of the show's final season on the air.

Throughout the series' duration, Robert Young and James Brolin worked well together and had a good rapport. Like many ambitious young actors, Brolin yearned to have as much time in the spotlight as possible and occasionally pushed to have his character play a more prominent role. Young was patient but firm in reproofing him. As daughter Carol put it, "At times, James thought he should be the star. Daddy reminded him that he wasn't."

His long exposure on *Welby* undoubtedly helped to bolster Brolin's subsequent career, which included many roles on television and in films. His TV roles included hotel manager Peter McDermott on *Hotel* (1983–1988), and John Short in *Life in Pieces* (2015–2019). For *Hotel*, he was nominated twice for Golden Globes for Best Performance by an Actor in a TV Series, but did not win.

He appeared in the films *Skyjacked* (1972), *Westworld* (1973), *Gable and Lombard* (1976), *Capricorn One* (1978), in which he costarred with Elliott Gould, *The Amityville Horror* (1979), and *Night of the Juggler* (1980). In 1983, he came this/close to becoming the next James Bond when Roger Moore (the British fellow) indicated that he wanted out, but at the last moment the producers persuaded Moore to continue.

Asked about his *Welby* role by a *Parade* interviewer, Brolin said that he auditioned for the role of Kiley and "I won it for the pilot episode. [It was] the prize of the year. I went from total obscurity bouncing around the Fox lot to Emmy-winning actor."

If his big and little screen successes were not enough, Brolin also had the good fortune to woo and wed singer-actress Barbara Streisand in 1998.

Welby was still enjoying favorable ratings in 1976, but the writers may have run out of illnesses that the doctors had not already dealt with. An episode titled "Vanity Case" involved a woman who is losing her vision, a less challenging problem than many the doctors had treated over the past six years. It was the final episode, airing in May, 1976.

———

For *Father Knows Best Reunion*, the cast visits on *Good Morning, America*. From Left: Jane Wyatt, Elinor Donahue, Robert Young, Billy Gray, Lauren Chapin; *Lauren Chapin collection*

For a time, Robert Young mostly declined any invitations he may have received to come out of retirement after the finale of *Marcus Welby, M.D.* There were a few exceptions. He did reunite with his television family for a TV movie special on NBC called *Father Knows Best Reunion*, which aired May 15, 1977. That was followed by another special on December 18, 1977, called *Father Knows Best: Home for Christmas*. By then Betty and Bud were married, with families of their own, and Kathy, the youngest, was engaged.

In 1980, Robert was briefly hospitalized for what was diagnosed as a drug dependency. How the doctors dealt with that is not known, but again he remained out of sight for a time.

In 1984, he donned his medical garb one more time for the TV movie special *The Return of Marcus Welby, M.D.*, which aired May 16. Rather than dealing with anyone's medical problem, this time he was trying to help mend the relationship between his old friend, the hospital administrator, and his estranged son.

Then in 1987, he took on a role that he felt he could not turn down. He starred in *Mercy or Murder?*, a television movie special based on the real life story of a man who killed his wife rather than watch her deteriorate from Alzheimer's disease and the bone disease osteoporosis. In a compelling portrayal of Roswell Gilbert, Young looks directly into the camera and asks the viewing audience what else could he do for his beloved Emily.

He later said that he felt a strong kinship with Gilbert because of his own long struggle with depression that left him feeling so desperate. At the time, he acknowledged another reason to an interviewer. "This is a strong, emotion-packed story," he said. "You don't get parts like this at seventy-nine — or at twenty-nine, for that matter."

After Robert's brief hospitalization in 1980, he appeared to have turned a corner. He seemed to have succeeded in ending his dependence on alcohol. He even hosted A.A. meetings in the Young home. Some adjustments in his medications may have helped, as did minimizing his performing activities. During the 1980s, his financial independence enabled him to limit his acting to a few roles of his choice.

In a 1983 interview, Robert said that after years of excessive drinking, he realized that it was leading him on a path to death. He said his struggle to stop was "an immensely slow, difficult process, but after slipping back again and again, I at last made a kind of giant step, and I was across the threshold to sanity."

Daughter Carol, on her own initiative, had joined the All Saints Church in Beverly Hills. Bob and Betty had long been Easter and Christmas churchgoers, but in deference to Carol they began attending and then became members. They got involved in church activities and Bob took on some leadership assignments. All these things seemed to have worked together to reduce his troubles and enable him to partake of a well-earned retirement with Elizabeth.

But late in the decade, Robert's physical and emotional problems flared up again. He had developed a heart problem and was dealing with early Alzheimer's disease. Daughter Kathy later remembered him saying that if things got too bleak, he and her mother would simply end it all together, but she assumed he was just having an especially bad day.

He did, indeed, have such a day on January 12, 1991. At their Westlake Village home, Bob and Betty Young had spent a good part of their day drinking together, and continued on into the evening. As Betty sat on a couch listening, and occasionally attempting a word of comfort, Bob paced up and down emoting about difficulties they both endured and for which there seemed no escape. In seeming desperation, he proposed that they form a suicide pact and kill themselves. Betty later recalled that she thought it was just a drunken ramble.

It was not. When she showed no sign of agreeing to his suggestion, Bob went outside and began rummaging in their garage. He found a garden hose and some black tape. In a fumbling effort, he was able to tape one end of the hose to the tailpipe of his car. He then ran the other end of the hose through the car window, got inside and turned the engine on.

What saved Bob's life was his limited knowledge of the workings of an automobile engine. Several times, he turned the key to start the car. Each time, it sputtered briefly, but the exhaust fumes could not be expelled quickly enough and the engine would die.

In what a sober person would have known was a foolish move, Bob stumbled back into the house and called his auto club to send a service truck. When the truck arrived, the mechanic quickly surmised what was happening and called the authorities.

Police and an ambulance soon arrived. A woozy Bob told the police, "I want to die. I'm too old and tired of living." He was instead taken to a hospital. Found almost unconscious inside on the couch, Betty was taken there also. She was found to be dehydrated and suffering from blood alcohol poisoning — three times the legal limit of intoxication. A double tragedy had been averted.

The incident was reported in *The National Enquirer* and made nationwide headlines. *The Enquirer* received more than 25,000 letters from readers who expressed their sympathies to both the Youngs, wished them a speedy recovery and offered prayers and encouragement.

Robert later responded in a letter printed in *The Enquirer*. He said, "It means very, very much to both me and Betty that the good people into whose homes I came each week for so many years still remember and care. I wish I could handwrite a note to each of you to express the gratitude I feel. Instead, perhaps this will let you know how deeply it cheered and heartened me! Thank YOU!"

After recovering from his initial emergency treatment, Robert voluntarily admitted himself to Thousand Oaks' Charter Hospital for psychiatric treatment and a thorough examination. It was then discovered that he suffered from a chemical imbalance, which probably was the cause of his chronic depression, or at least a significant contributing factor. He was at last able to be treated with medication that gave some relief.

Robert then went public about his problems, speaking candidly about them and encouraging others with similar problems to seek help. Daughter Carol noted that alcoholism and depression are subjects often avoided, but she said, "Daddy realized a lot could be learned through his being open and showing you can get through these things." She also recalled that her father seemed to have an increased appreciation of life and the importance of his family.

Having supported each other in their respective battles with depression and alcoholism, Robert and Elizabeth now stayed close to home, living quietly for the most part. Elizabeth's health had been failing. On April 4, 1994, she died, just three days past her eighty-fourth birthday. She was interred in the Graceland section of Forest Lawn Memorial Park in Glendale.

Robert's health was in decline by this time. In his late 80s, his personal doctor had detected that he had a heart problem. He had since been diagnosed as being in the early stage of Alzheimer's disease, but symptoms were minor. He was mostly homebound. His four daughters and their families visited often. He had a staff of people for housekeeping, cooking and care of the property. A couple named John and Gayle Fredericks had become his full-time caregivers.

For his ninetieth birthday, in 1997, the family arranged for a birthday party attended by many of his friends from movie and television days. Jane Wyatt, Elinor Donahue, and Billy Gray all attended.

The Fredericks assisted Robert to an easy chair in the den, where some lights and a video camera had been set up. Each guest came in to sit beside Robert for a very brief chat that was captured on film. Robert seemed alert and put on a good show of cheerfulness.

Outside after, it was a somber parting for Wyatt, Donahue, and Gray, as they realized that this might be their last contact with their fellow performer and dear friend.

Elinor, however, lived in the area. About two months later, she received a call from the Fredericks telling her that Robert was having a very "up" day and inviting her to come visit. She did. It was a brief but lovely visit. Holding Robert's hand as he lay in bed, she told him how much she loved him. He smiled and said, "I love you, too." She leaned over to kiss his cheek and Robert raised her hand to his lips to kiss it. Then he closed his eyes, letting her know that he was tired. She said, "Goodbye," and quietly left the room, feeling blessed to have had one more very personal visit with the man she could never call "Daddy."

At ninety-one, Robert was frail and quiet, but generally in good spirits and aware of his surroundings. At the Westlake Village home that he and Elizabeth called "the Enchanted Cottage," he died quietly of respiratory failure on July 21, 1998.

Daughter Betty said, "When I saw Dad a couple of days ago, he was alert and joking. We had a wonderful visit."

Robert Young was survived by his four daughters, six grandchildren, and two great-grandchildren. He was buried at Forest Lawn Memorial Park in Glendale, beside Elizabeth, his beloved wife of sixty-one years.

For the gentle, fatherly man who had endured so much inner turmoil, peace at last.

FATHER'S FAMILY: WHO WERE THOSE PEOPLE?

No one could have personified the head of the Anderson family better than Robert Young. Yet *Father Knows Best* would not have enjoyed such a faithful audience had he not been accompanied by two sets of talented cast members. To do justice to all of them would require another book, but what follows is a brief recognition of the folk who made up *Father's* two families.

The Radio Family

Born in Amesbury, Massachusetts, June Whitley (August 26, 1921 - May 25, 2006) was the first Margaret Anderson on radio. She also was a featured player on *Deadline Mystery*, a crime drama with a newspaper background that aired on ABC for just one season in 1947. It seems her main focus was to become a film actress, and she did find her way into a number of small roles, mostly uncredited.

Though she didn't attain stardom, she later found her niche in television. She appeared in such diverse series as *Mr. & Mrs. North*, *I Love Lucy*, *Dragnet*, *The Monkees*, *Mannix*, *The Flying Nun*, *The Rockford Files*, *Wonder Woman*, *The Donna Reed Show*, *The Lone Ranger*, *The Incredible Hulk*, *Little House on the Prairie* and *Alice*.

In 1977, she had a small role in the television special *Father Knows Best: Home for Christmas*. She sometimes performed using her married name of June Whitley Taylor, including four episodes in which she appeared as a nurse on *Marcus Welby, M.D.* Among her last screen appearances were small roles in the TV films *Delta County USA*, *Rescue from Gilligan's Island*, *The Place to Be*, and a more noticeable supporting role in the 1979 mini-series *Women in White*. In all of these she used her married name.

After ending her acting career, June Whitley became a long-time volunteer with the American Red Cross and an active member of the Federal Emergency Management Agency until her retirement in 2005.

———

When June Whitley left *Father* at the end of the second season, she was replaced by Dorothy Lovett (February 16, 1915 - April 28, 1998). Born in Providence, Rhode Island, Lovett got her start in radio on local programs that included a cooking program, a shopping service and a weekly fashion show (on radio?). She later graduated to playing Toni Sherwood on *Rocky Jordan* (1945-1947), Jan Carter on *Guiding Light* (1948-1949), and Grace Adam on *The Seeking Heart* (1953-1955). In 1954, she began playing Adam on the television version of the show.

She also performed periodically on *Lux Radio Theatre* and *Doctor Christian*. The latter was a natural casting for her, as she had starred as Nurse Judy Price in five films about the doctor between 1939 and 1941. Under contract to RKO, she was loaned to Universal Studios for a role in *The Green Hornet Strikes Again*. Lovett also had a small part in *Look Who's Laughing*, with Edgar Bergen, Charlie McCarthy, and Fibber McGee and Molly. Her last screen appearance was a small role in 1965's *A Patch of Blue*.

Jean Vander Pyl (October 11, 1919 - April 10, 1999) assumed the role of Margaret Anderson in the show's fourth season and continued for its duration. She was born in Philadelphia, but her father was a salesman, and the family moved several times, eventually settling in Los Angeles. She graduated from Beverly Hills High School in 1937. Having played Juliet in a citywide Shakespeare festival, she decided that she wanted to be an actress and attended UCLA as an acting student. While still an undergraduate, she got her first job at a local radio station playing damsels in distress on a drama series, *Calling All Cars.*

An illness led her to decide that the stage was not her destination. Radio afforded many opportunities without physical and wardrobe requirements. She soon was performing on such programs as *Lux Radio Theatre, The Cavalcade of America, Chandu the Magician*, and *Family Theatre*. She frequently made incidental appearances as various characters on *The Joan Davis Show, Fibber McGee and Molly, The Alan Young Show, My Favorite Husband*, and *The Halls of Ivy*. Her vocal versatility even enabled her to play numerous girlfriends who came and went in the life of Andrew Brown on *Amos 'n' Andy*.

Vander Pyl did manage to make the shift to television and appeared in a number of popular series. However, she is best remembered, if only her voice, as Wilma Flintstone in the immensely popular series *The Flintstones*. She had the good fortune to be available and chosen to do character voices when the fledgling Hanna-Barbera studios began producing such series as *Huckleberry Hound, Quick Draw McGraw, Yogi Bear* and *Top Cat*. Then came *The Flintstones* and her role as Wilma. The show ran on ABC-TV from 1960 to 1966 and in countless follow-up incarnations.

When the show went off the air, Jean accepted a lump sum payment of $15,000 in lieu of residuals. In 1995, she told an interviewer, "If I was getting residuals, I wouldn't live in San Clemente. I'd *own* San Clemente."

Rehearsing for their vocal roles on *The Flintstones*, from right, Alan Reed, Jean Vander Pyl, Bea Benaderet, Mel Blanc; *Nostalgia Digest collection*

Vander Pyl was a life-long smoker and died of lung cancer. Her Wilma character was notable for a sort of closed-mouth giggle. Her son told a reporter that she and the Hanna-Barbera people adopted the giggle because if she laughed out loud she would have a coughing fit.

Kathy, the youngest of the Anderson children, was played by Norma Jean Nilsson for the first three years. Born on New Year's Day 1938, she was perhaps destined to be a child star. She had a lovely singing voice and perfect pitch. Her mother was Swedish and a piano teacher, so Norma became bi-lingual and a pianist.

She was but four years old when she won a talent contest on Los Angeles radio station KECA. During World War II, she participated in groups that entertained troops at camps around the United States. She was especially pleased to be on *The Bob Hope Show* for a remote broadcast from one camp.

At five, Norma Jean made what she later called her "first big-time radio appearance," playing a terminally ill girl on *Free World Theatre*. Her picture adorned the cover of *Radio Life* magazine in

1946. In 1947, she was the highest-paid child actress in radio. Not surprising, as she recently had scored 162 on an IQ test. An impressive score at any age, since it indicated that she was smarter than 99% of the rest of us. In 1951, *Radio and Television Mirror* magazine reported that she was now a member of the Five Hundred Club, a group of child actors who had appeared in five hundred or more radio broadcasts.

In addition to her role as Kathy, Norma Jean played daughter Cookie Bumstead on *Blondie* and "the little girl who lives next door" on *The Jack Carson Show*. She also was heard on *Suspense, Luke Slaughter of Tombstone, Cavalcade of America,* and the radio version of *Have Gun, Will Travel*.

Kathy once enthused to a reporter that she especially enjoyed being in the *Father Knows Best* cast because Robert Young made rehearsals so much fun. "Maybe he'll spin me around in a quick waltz," she said, "or sometimes he'll tease us all day long. Other times he'll join us at the piano for impromptu singing. He takes part in all our doings, and makes us enjoy them more."

As *Father Knows Best* prepared to begin its fourth season, Norma Jean Nilsson was fourteen years old and decided to move on. The role of Kathy Anderson was assumed by nine-year-old Helen Strohm, and she continued in the part for the remainder of the show's radio run.

Strohm is a bit of a mystery woman — or girl. Presumably, she must have had some previous radio experience. She surely did not just walk into the studio and announce, "I'm available." Yet the usual sources make no mention of any other radio programs on which she performed, either as a regular or occasional incidental appearances. Even John Dunning's book *On the Air,*

a virtual encyclopedia of old-time radio, cites no other radio role for Strohm.

Several sources mention that she had some exposure in films without citing titles. In all likelihood, they were minor roles, probably uncredited. One source does mention that her last role was as a young girl, again likely uncredited, in the 1953 slapstick space-comedy *Abbott and Costello Go to Mars*.

None of the usual sources seem to have any clue as to what became of Helen Strohm after that. Given her age, it's possible she may still be with us, but that, too, is a mystery.

———

Ted Donaldson took on the role of James Jr., "Bud," and continued for the entire run of *Father Knows Best* on radio. Born in Brooklyn on August 20, 1933, he was the son of singer-composer Will Donaldson. His mother died when he was four and his father married organist and composer Muriel Pollock. When he was old enough for school, they enrolled him at the Professional Children's School in New York City.

In 1937, he made his debut on an NBC radio show. By 1941, he had graduated to playing Tiny Tim in a week-long serialized presentation of *A Christmas Carol* on *Wheatena Playhouse*. That same year, he played young Harlan Day in a stage production of *Life with Father*. In 1943, he shared the stage with Gregory Peck in *Sons and Soldiers*.

The next year, he won a small role in *Mr. Winkle Goes to War*, a Columbia Pictures film starring Edward G. Robinson. Columbia liked what they saw and signed him to a contract. He then shared star billing with Cary Grant and Janet Blair in 1944's comedy-fantasy *Once Upon a Time*. On loan to 20th Century-Fox, he appeared in 1945's Oscar-nominated *A Tree Grows in Brooklyn*.

Though not overworked, Donaldson kept busy during the 1940s in such films as *A Guy, a Gal, and a Pal* (1945), *The Red Stallion* (1947), and a title role in Warner Bros.' *The Decision of Christopher Blake* (1948). During the 1940s, Columbia featured Ted in a series of "*Rusty*" films about a boy and his dog. For whatever reason, they did not prove as popular with moviegoers as did the films of Lassie or Rin Tin Tin. He had already been transitioning into television roles when he made his last big screen appearance along with Shelley Winters in 1952's *Phone Call from a Stranger*.

Ted might have taken his role of Bud Anderson to the television adaptation of *Father Knows Best*, but he was full-grown and yearning for more adult roles. Unfortunately, few were forthcoming, and he soon retired from acting. Years later, he told an interviewer that it was "one of the two or three most stupid things that I have done, because not only would the salary have been very nice for five years, but the residuals would have also."

———

Rhoda Williams (July 19, 1930 – March 8 2006) became daughter Betty, the oldest of the Anderson children. She was born in Denver, Colorado, but her family later moved to Galveston, Texas, and then to Hollywood, California. At the age of five, she began performing small parts on local radio and soon had her own show, *We Who Are Young*, on station KMEC. Thanks to her ability to modulate her young voice, she got her first network role playing a small boy on NBC's *I Want a Divorce*. She soon began appearing on such programs as *Dr. Christian*, *One Man's Family*, *The Life of Riley*, and *Lux Radio Theatre*.

No slacker as a student, she was just fourteen when she graduated from Hollywood High School. She then went on to receive a bachelor's degree from UCLA when she was eighteen. In 1972, she earned a master's degree in theatre from California State University. She later taught speech and voice classes.

Though she did not attain star status, she appeared in numerous films. Among them: *National Velvet* (1944), *The Corn Is Green* (1945), *Our Vines Have Tender Grapes* (1945), *That Haven Girl* (1947), *House of Strangers* (1949), *The Heart Is a Rebel* (1958), and *The Sergeant Was a Lady* (1961). As a voice actress, she was the evil stepsister Drizella in Walt Disney's 1950 classic *Cinderella*. She also provided a dubbed-in voice for Brigitte Bardot in the American release of *The Night Heaven Fell* and alien voices for *Star Trek IV* and *Star Trek V*.

As radio gave way to television, Rhoda appeared on *The Big Valley*, *Ironside*, *The Twilight Zone*, *Police Woman*, *General Hospital*, *Barnaby Jones*, *The Dick Van Dyke Show*, *Felony Squad*, *Laredo*, *Dragnet*, and *The Jimmy Stewart Show*. She even rejoined Robert Young for a guest appearance on *Marcus Welby, M.D.*

Williams joined both the Screen Actors Guild and AFTRA (the American Federation of Television and Radio Artists) in 1938. She served on the Los Angeles board of AFTRA and at times was secretary and then president of the Los Angeles Chapter of the Coalition of Labor Union Women.

On *Father Knows Best*, Mary Lee Robb (niece Marjorie on *The Great Gildersleeve*) occasionally filled in for Rhoda, but Rhoda otherwise played Betty for the entire run of the program on radio.

Rhoda Williams had been a resident of Eugene, Oregon, for fourteen years when she died of cardiac arrest. She was survived by David Van Meter, her husband of forty-four years, two daughters, two sons, twelve grandchildren, and three great-grandchildren.

The Television Family

Jane Waddington Wyatt (August 12, 1910 - October 20, 2006), born in Campgaw, New Jersey, was a descendant on her mother's side of the Dutch van Renssalaer families that began settling in the Colonies as early as 1638. At one time, they owned much of what is now New York City. The state's Renssalaer County is named after them. She attended the exclusive Chapin School and went on to Barnard College. After two years, she left to join an apprentice program at the Berkshire Playhouse in Stockbridge, Massachusetts.

For six months she filled various roles before her first New York stage appearance in 1931's *Give Me Yesterday*. In 1933, she succeeded Margaret Sullivan in *Dinner at Eight* on Broadway. The following year, she was lured to Hollywood for her film debut in *One More River*, which earned her a contract with Universal Pictures. She then was in three more films, including 1934's *Great Expectations*. In 1937, on loan to Columbia Pictures, she costarred in Frank Capra's production of *Lost Horizon*, playing the young Shangri-la beauty who enchants Ronald Colman.

She took time off in November of 1935 to marry investment broker Edgar Ward. Their marriage produced two sons, Christopher and Michael, and lasted until Edgar died on November 8, 2000, just one day short of their sixty-fifth wedding anniversary. Because her family was in New York, and because she preferred New York to Hollywood, she commuted frequently, doing more stage work than films. In 1945, she appeared on Broadway opposite Franchot Tone in *Hope for the Best*.

Wyatt's understated beauty made her popular with both male and female moviegoers. Although she never achieved super star status in films, she appeared in more than two dozen through the 1950s. In most, she either had a starring role or a strong supporting part. Her costars included Cary Grant in *None But the Lonely Heart* (1944), Gregory Peck in *Gentleman's Agreement* (1947), Dana Andrews in *Boomerang* (1947), Dick Powell in *Pitfall* (1948), and Gary Cooper in *Task Force* (1949).

Wyatt's career suffered in the 1950s due to her outspoken opposition to Senator Joseph McCarthy. His headline-seeking anti-communist investigation caused many actors, writers and other Hollywood workers to be blacklisted. Wyatt said she was never a member of the Communist party, but was accused of a string of un-American activities, including being "prematurely anti-fascist" and advocating a second front against the Nazis. "I don't know why that was held against me," she said, "because [President] Roosevelt was [doing] the same thing." At one point, she joined Humphrey Bogart, Lauren Bacall and other Hollywood stars on a visit to Washington to confront McCarthy on his home turf.

During her years on *Father Knows Best,* her time at home was more limited but also more precious. On the set, she agreed with other cast members that they came to feel like family. Jane said that she became close with Elinor Donahue, Billy Gray, and Lauren Chapin, but not like a pseudo-mother. "Our relationship was more like a favorite aunt with her favorite nieces and nephew," she said. "I didn't feel the terrible responsibility that a real mother feels for her children." As for those who criticized the series as too idealistic, she responded, "We can't have it exactly like real life. It would be too boring. We thought it was life as we wanted it to be."

When the series ended, Jane continued working on a number of television programs. She appeared in such diverse series as *Wagon Train, The Alfred Hitchcock Hour, Here Come the Brides,* and *The Virginian.* She had supporting roles in eight made-for-TV films. Late in her career, she had a recurring role in the 1980s medical drama *St. Elsewhere,* as Katherine Auschlander, wife of hospital administrator Dr. Daniel Auschlander (Norman Lloyd).

From 1950 through 1986, Wyatt made just ten more scattered big screen appearances. The last was as Amanda Grayson, Spock's mother, in the 1986 film *Star Trek IV: The Voyage Home.* It was a reprise of a role she had played in a 1967 episode of the original NBC series. She once noted with amusement that the cameo appearances resulted in more fan mail than anything else she had done. She recalled once getting off a plane and hearing someone shout, "Amanda!" She looked around to see who Amanda was.

Speaking of fan mail, well into her nineties Jane never would refuse an autograph request from a fan, and spent much time meticulously answering her fan mail. She was a member of the Academy of Motion Picture Arts and Sciences (AMPAS), and a valuable supporter and member of the March of Dimes from its inception in 1943. In 1986, she received the Women's International Center (WIC) Living Legacy Award.

During the 1990s, though she made no formal announcement, Jane considered herself retired. She turned down the role of Old Rose in the film *Titanic* (1997) to remain so. She spent her later years at home with her family, and was rarely seen in public. In 1998, at age eighty, she said goodbye to her long-time friend and costar Robert Young after the beloved actor died at age ninety-one. She attended his funeral along with her television son, Billy Gray.

Wyatt died of natural causes at her home in Bel Air, California, on October 20, 2006, at the age of ninety-six. She was interred with her husband Edgar Bethune Ward at San Fernando Mission Cemetery in Mission Hills, CA. She was survived by her sons, Christopher and Michael, three grandchildren, and five great-grandchildren.

Jane Wyatt has a Star on the Hollywood Walk of Fame at 6350 Hollywood Blvd.

———

Lauren Ann Chapin, who became daughter Kathy "Kitten" Anderson, was born on May 23, 1945, in Los Angeles, California. She was the third child of Roy and Marquerite "Megs" Chapin. Brothers Mike and Billy were eleven and two years old.

Lauren's childhood at home was an extreme opposite of the idealized family life of *Father Knows Best*. Her mother married a man who came from a wealthy family, but she was distressed to learn that they expected him to earn his own living. Their marriage was already in trouble before Lauren reached school age. After she was molested by her father and told her mother, they were divorced.

Living in Los Angeles, Megs Chapin had many friends who worked in various capacities for Hollywood film studios. With their advice and knowledge of openings, she was able to get both Mike, and later Billy, started as child actors. Groomed and rehearsed by their mother, they were successful in obtaining many roles in both movies and radio, and later television. What they earned became a major portion of the family's income, and Megs became what is often called a backstage mother.

As Lauren was growing up, her mother was focused on the boys' film work and paid her little mind. Lauren later concluded that Mother was lacking in the ability to show affection. For that, Lauren relied more on a lady named Sterling, a large, Black woman who was their full-time "nanny." When she was school age, Mother enrolled her in a convent school where she was housed during the week, returning home only on weekends.

Lauren's mother evidently did not deem her capable of following in her two brothers' footsteps. Not until an acquaintance who was a studio agent alerted her to a search for a girl that sounded just right for Lauren. A series of contacts with various people led to Lauren's interview and reading with Eugene Rodney.

Blessed with a talent for memorizing, Lauren had often learned songs and poems that she used to entertain company. As she got a little older, she was able to memorize the lyrics to all the popular tunes she heard and enjoyed. Given a script in advance and told to learn Kathy's lines, she in fact memorized the lines of all the characters.

When she entered Eugene Rodney's office, he was chomping on a smelly cigar. He checked her name on his list, steered her to a chair, and said he would read the other characters' parts and she would come in with her Kathy lines. Lauren bravely spoke up and said she would do better if she could do all the other lines except Father, and let him read those.

Rodney raised a doubtful eyebrow but agreed and said, "Anything else?"

"Yes," Lauren replied. "If you're going to be my father, you can't be smoking that smelly cigar." Rodney snubbed out the cigar in an ash tray and they began.

When they finished without a falter, Lauren knew she had done well. Rodney thanked her and said they would get back to her if she was chosen as a finalist. As mentioned earlier, she was one of ten girls who did screen tests, and Robert Young himself chose her.

A whole new life opened up for Lauren on the set of *Father Knows Best*. Robert Young adopted all the youngsters and treated Lauren like his own daughter. Director William Russell was patient and helpful with all the young cast members. Lauren became part of what, for her, was a second family.

For Lauren, life on the set of *Father Knows Best* became a respite from reality. At home, her mother kept her well dressed and groomed and felt that this was enough to express her love and expect love in return. She could not comprehend that Lauren yearned to dress like her girlfriends, in jeans and bobby sox. Lauren took to changing clothes after leaving the house, often eating with friends' families and coming home late.

When brother Mike was old enough, he left home and struck out on his own. Brother Billy was finding steady work in numerous movie roles and sometimes resented that Lauren was now receiving more attention. Mother's social drinking had developed into an alcohol problem. Lauren often came home to find her asleep on the couch with an empty glass or bottle nearby.

Although Lauren was now bringing home a substantial portion of the family's income, she was not given an allowance. She took to sneaking money from Mother's purse before going out to meet her friends.

Her hours with the television cast and crew were for Lauren an escape from a life in which she felt trapped and unloved. One of the saddest days of your young life was the day that she came to the studio gate and the guard told her that he could not let her in. The show was winding down for its final season, but things were cut short by a writers' strike. The most recently canned episode would be the last, and there would be no farewell party.

Having become so recognized as the young Anderson daughter, Lauren found that there was a dearth of other roles open to her. Relations with her mother did not improve. At sixteen, Lauren left home, dropped out of school, and began struggling to make it on her own with a series of short-lived jobs. She made some bad friends and began drinking and popping pills.

Before a year was out, she was married. It was the first of three marriages. One would be annulled and the others ended in divorce. They did, however, produce two children, son Mathew and daughter Summer.

She struggled with both her alcohol and drug use, at times selling drugs — and even her body — to support her habit. On one occasion, she was arrested for drug possession. In lieu of a prison sentence, she was sent to a mental health institute where they sought to rehabilitate drug users. When free, she found what work she could to support her children. She was at times a cocktail waitress, a dog groomer, even a flight attendant. She worked for an insurance company, a brokerage firm, and a financial institution. She even learned to be a midwife and assisted natural childbirths in hospitals.

In 1977, she was thrilled but nervous when invited to participate in the made-for-TV special *Father Knows Best Reunion*. She knew that the cast and crew would have heard of her various troubles and she dreaded facing them. But she bravely returned to the familiar set. On entering her dressing room she found it swathed in roses. Taped to her mirror was a note that said: "Welcome back, Kitten. We all love you." Robert, Jane, Elinor, and Billy all gave her big warm hugs. It was like a real family reunion. And it was no less joyful when she returned for the next special, *Father Knows Best: Home for Christmas*.

In 1979, while recovering from viral encephalitis, she hesitantly agreed to a sincere and earnest friend's invitation to come to church with her. It was a dramatic turning point in her life. She was greeted with warmth by numerous complete strangers in the congregation and listened to an impassioned sermon that stirred her heart. When it was over and those suffering physical or other troubles were invited to come forward, she was one of the first up front.

Her conversion and return to church led her to become an ordained evangelist, and she sometimes leads tours in the Holy Land. She found her way back into the entertainment world managing singers and actors.

Chapin actively supports several charities benefiting underprivileged and abused children. Her work has earned her the title "Honorary Mayor" in several cities.

Though she never reconciled with her mother, she realized years later that Mother was a sick woman. Much of the money that her children brought in paid for fancy houses and new cars. Lauren said, "My mother didn't know how to save, but she spent very well." From her years on *Father Knows Best*, Lauren received only $19,000 that had been set aside in savings bonds bearing her name.

In 1989, Lauren made periodic appearances on a number of television shows to promote a book she wrote about her troubled life and her spiritual revival. The book was aptly titled *Father Does Know Best*.

While Kathy "Kitten" Anderson enjoyed the model
family on the TV hit "Father Knows Best," young actress
Lauren Chapin suffered the agony of an abusive home.
After TV fame passed, her off-screen life kept spiraling
downward until she found the Father
who had cared all along...
Father Does Know Best
The Lauren Chapin Story
LAUREN CHAPIN
with ANDREW COLLINS

William Thomas Gray was born in Los Angeles on January 13, 1938, the son of William and Beatrice Gray. His mother was a successful actress. One day when he was five, his mother was on stage rehearsing a play and Billy was running up and down the aisles. His mother's agent was watching from the rear. She took Billy up front and told Beatrice, "I can put this kid to work." Mom nodded and said, "Go for it."

Young Billy soon began filling a string of small parts. They were all uncredited, with few or no spoken lines, but between 1943 and 1949, he appeared in more than thirty mostly forgettable films. In 1949, he and his mother both had small unrelated parts in *Abbott and Costello Meet the Killer, Boris Karloff.*

"It was weird," Billy once told an interviewer. It seemed that every part he tried out for, he got. "I was a kid. I hardly got any lines at first, [but] the roles kept coming and the lines got longer."

Even if anonymously, Billy appeared on the screen with numerous big name stars. He was in 1945's *The Adventures of Rusty* (the first of the series starring Ted Donaldson). In 1950, he appeared with Jack Carson and Lola Albright in *The Good Humor Man* and had a memorable (for him) scene with Humphrey Bogart in *In a Lonely Place*. He remembered Bogart as taking his work very seriously and being very unpretentious as a star.

He saddled up out West (or up North?) with Gene Autry and Pat Buttram for 1951's *Gene Autry and the Mounties*. That year, he also joined Burt Lancaster in *Jim Thorpe-All-American*, playing the Native American athlete as a boy, and was just twelve years younger than Patricia Neal when he played her son in *The Day the Earth Stood Still*. In the latter, he had some chipper dialogue peppered with a lot of "Gee's" and "Aw, Mom's."

He especially enjoyed working with Doris Day in 1951's *On Moonlight Bay*. Asked about her, Billy said she was "absolutely lovely. She was incredibly charming, outgoing, and just sweet to everyone on the set. She was truly wonderful."

Still playing youngsters, in 1952 Billy was one of the Kettle boys in *Ma and Pa Kettle at the Fair* with Marjorie Main and Percy Kilbride. He was a teenaged Bryan Foy in 1955's *The Seven Little Foys*, starring Bob Hope. The basic storyline notwithstanding, the picture's major highlight was a tabletop dance competition between Hope as father Eddie Foy and James Cagney as George M. Cohan.

In 1953, Billy got his first motorcycle, a 500cc Matchless British racing bike. It was the beginning of a love affair that lasted far into his adult years. As mentioned previously, he rode to the *Father Knows Best* studio on his bike. That was okay with the producers, but they curtailed him from participating in weekend drag races lest they find themselves without a prime cast member.

Billy's short stature — he peaked at 5 feet, 6½ inches — enabled him to continue portraying the sixteenish James Jr. when he was of voting age. In 1959, the role got him nominated for an Emmy for Outstanding Supporting Actor (Continuing Character) in a Comedy Series. He lost out to the versatile Tom Poston, possibly because Poston was long overdue to be thus recognized.

Like many of his contemporaries, Billy Gray discovered marijuana while still a teenager. He became a regular user, but in manageable proportions. Nevertheless, the weed was illegal everywhere at the time. Its use even was condemned in an extreme message film titled *Reefer Madness*.

One day in 1962, as he was parking his car, an officer came to his window, sniffed, and asked Billy to get out. Though he had not been smoking, Billy had a stash under the seat. He was arrested for possession. He pleaded nolo contendere, meaning he was guilty without officially admitting it. His sentence could have been for as much as ten years, but for whatever reason he served forty-five days and was released.

Film roles all but dried up after that. But his years on *Father Knows Best* had afforded him an inroad on television. He already had appeared on *Peter Gunn*, *Bachelor Father*, *The Deputy*, *General Electric Theatre*, *Alfred Hitchcock Presents*, *The Red Skelton Hour*, and other series. For the remainder of the 1960s, he was able to continue finding incidental roles on such series as *Arrest and Trial*, *The Greatest Show on Earth*, *Rawhide*, *Combat*, *Medical Center*, *The Bold Ones*, and others.

In 1964, he made a brief return to the live stage. At the Cape Playhouse in Dennis, Massachusetts, he appeared in the Joseph Stein play *Enter Laughing* with Lynn Bari and Alan Mowbray.

During the 1970s, Billy had minor roles in a handful of minor films. One exception was his appearance in 1979's *Love and Bullets*, in which he joined Charles Bronson, Jill Ireland, and Rod Steiger. Perhaps because he was playing a cop, he used the name William Gray in the film's credits.

His reprise of his Bud role in the two 1977 *Father Knows Best* specials had to be both a joyful and nostalgic experience. Like Lauren Chapin, he was welcomed back with no reservations, and the cast was again like an almost real, loving family. Billy recalled that in that family atmosphere he had become very good friends with Jane Wyatt. The fact that she was a devout Roman Catholic and he a professed atheist once led to them having a long, deep discussion about religion.

Billy Gray's departure from acting opened a whole new vista to him. He became a competitive Class A Speedway motorcycle racer from 1970 until 1995. His bike became known as the "Orange Crate Special," a name given to it by the announcer at the Irwindale Raceway because of the solid orange rims that Billy used. A video of one of his races can be viewed on his website, *billygray.com*. (Caution: Not for the faint-hearted.)

From his early boyhood years, Billy has had a penchant for taking things apart to see how they work. He was always able to reassemble them, but as he got older he often found ways to make them work better. He once designed a candleholder to go inside jack-o-lanterns. It sold over seven million units.

He also invented a device called the Hose KlipÔ for deck fills on boats. It snaps over any standard hose, and the compression fitting holds the hose in place and prevents it from popping out of the deck fill during filling. It was so successful that he was honored by the IBEX Innovation Awards, the largest technical trade event in North America for marine industry professionals.

Now that his film and racing days are over, Billy is co-owner of a company called BigRock Manufacturing (website *BigrockMFG. com*). In addition to mechanical devices, they sell a number of music-related items, including Billy's F1 Pick, the "only tunable guitar pick," and other items beyond this writer's comprehension.

During his time playing Bud Anderson, Billy was renting a basement apartment for $75.00 a month. Thanks to his tenure on

Father Knows Best, he now owns the house. Its size enabled him to convert part of it into a machine shop and a storage area for assorted bent parts.

In spite of some twists and turns, Billy Gray professes that he has mostly enjoyed his life, and he has few regrets. Musing about his acting and racing careers, he says he'd nonetheless like his tombstone to say "Toolmaker."

———

Mary Eleanor Donahue was born in Tacoma, Washington, on April 19, 1937, the daughter of Thomas and Doris Donahue. Her mother perhaps had a premonition that she would become a performer, for she was enrolled in tap dancing class at just eighteen months. The classes were in the same building as a local radio station. Eleanor had a talent for learning and singing popular tunes, and the station had a Saturday morning program that featured young performers. At the age of two, she became one of them, and was on the program for three years.

She continued her dancing lessons, with a focus on ballet. While still a preschooler, she spent time on the Best Terry Vaudeville circuit. Touring Spokane, Yakima, Seattle and other

Pacific Northwest theaters, she had a "single" act, singing and dancing.

By the time she was five, she was under contract to Universal Studios as a child actress. In her early roles, her parts were sometimes small, but she got to say a few lines and her name appeared in the credits. She got to share the screen, however briefly, with many of the day's popular stars. In 1943, she appeared with bandleader Ozzie Nelson and his off-screen wife Harriett Hilliard in the musical comedy *Honeymoon Lodge*, and with Donald O'Conner in *Mister Big*.

In the latter, her role of Mugsy was going to be written out because the producers couldn't find anyone the right size with the talent to play her. A family friend recommended Eleanor, she was asked to dance a little and say a few lines, and she was hired. Eleanor was a big fan of Donald O'Conner, and it was a thrill when they met and he gave her a big hug.

In 1944's *Bowery to Broadway*, showcasing the singing talent of Maria Montez, she again kept company with Donald O'Conner, and also with Jack Oakie. Her role was that of Ann Blyth as a child. She fondly remembers doing a dance school scene that sets up Blyth's character's singing career. That same year, surrounded by Alan Ladd, Loretta Young, and Susan Hayward, she managed to look like a four-year-old in *And Now Tomorrow*.

In 1946, Eleanor was loaned out to Republic Pictures for *Winter Wonderland*. Having moved to MGM, she was in her element in *The Unfinished Dance* (1947), a film about members of a ballet company. In that one she rubbed elbows with Cyd Charisse and the child star Margaret O'Brien. She was one of the *Three Daring Daughters* in the 1948 Technicolor musical starring Jeanette MacDonald, Jose Iturbi, and Jane Powell.

After 1948's *Tenth Avenue Angel* there was a brief pause between films and she used it to do a make-over of her screen name. Having felt for a time that her name was too lengthy, she happened to read an article by British writer Elinor Glynn. She liked the spelling of Elinor. When attached to her own last name, minus her birth name of Mary, she felt it had a nice ring to it. (See above.) With a nod of approval from her mother, she became Elinor Donahue.

The Happy Years followed in 1950, and *Tea for Two*, a rehash of the 1925 stage musical *No, No, Nanette*. She especially enjoyed doing the latter, even though she probably was easy to miss among its stars, including Doris Day, Gordon MacRae, Eve Arden and Billy De Wolfe. During 1953-1954, she was a musical judge on ABC's *Jukebox Jury.*

Elinor's parents were divorced when she was seven years old. Her mother had little work experience but took what jobs she could find, including making ballet costumes and being a wrapper at the May Company during the holidays. Although she did not achieve stardom on the big screen, Elinor's steady work in films provided the main source of income for her mother and her.

In 1954, when she had her frustrating experience trying out for the role of daughter Betty on *Father Knows Best*, she came home to tell her mother, "Let's get on with our lives. I don't want to discuss this!" It was, then, a joy to learn that she'd won the part.

At sixteen, she was a pretty young lady, but much quieter than the character she was to play, even a bit shy. But Robert, Eugene Rodney, director William Russell, and the other cast members made her to feel as if she were being adopted into a close-knit family. Her years on the program were among the most enjoyable and memorable of her acting career. In 1959, she was nominated for an Emmy Award as Best Supporting Actress (Continuing Character) in a Comedy Series. She lost out to Ann Bradford Davis. Davis won for her role on *The Bob Cummings Show*, but she probably is best remembered as housekeeper Alice Nelson on *The Brady Bunch.*

Elinor recalls an occasion when her dancing skills saved the day. The script called for Betty to take ballet lessons and Rodney said they would have to find a lookalike dancer to fill in for Elinor. She said, "No need," and perfectly executed a few entrechats. Rodney was pleasantly surprised and they went on with the shoot.

During breaks between seasons on *Father Knows Best*, Elinor took great pleasure in doing some live stage work. In towns as far away as Missouri and Illinois, she performed in *George Washington Slept Here*, *Any Wednesday*, *The Pleasure of His Company*, *Picnic*, *Harvey*, and *Bell, Book, and Candle*, among other productions.

Like the other cast members, Elinor understood why *Father Knows Best* ended, but she couldn't help having a little "what if?" regret. However, while portraying Father's "Princess," she had made incidental appearances on other television programs, including *The Ray Bolger Show, U.S. Marshal,* and *The George Burns and Gracie Allen Show.* She was prepared to move on.

Freed from the demands of the series, she signed a three-year contract to appear on *The Andy Griffith Show.* She was cast as pharmacist Ellie Walker, and her name appeared in the show's opening credits. She became Andy's girlfriend, with the intent that if the two clicked with audiences they might even be married.

But in real life she had married when she was just nineteen, and it did not go well. The marriage ended in divorce in 1960. Dealing with the distress that led up to the divorce, Elinor requested and was granted a release from her contract after the 1960-1961 season.

She pulled her life together after that and began appearing in numerous television programs. During the remainder of the 1960s, she was seen on *77 Sunset Strip, Have Gun-Will Travel, Dr, Kildare, The Virginian, A Man Called Shenandoah, Star Trek,* and other series.

In the mid-1960s, she enjoyed a feature role as Joan Randall, the daughter of Walter Burnley (John McGiver) in the sitcom *Many Happy Returns,* about the complaint department of a Los Angeles department store. Between 1968 and 1970, she made three appearances as Dr. Jennifer Ethrington on *The Flying Nun,* and miraculously transformed herself into the sister of Sister Bertrille (Sally Field) on three other occasions.

During the 1970s, Donahue made frequent appearances as Miriam Welby (no relation to Marcus) on *The Odd Couple.* In the third season, she became the girlfriend of Felix Unger (Tony Randall) and made frequent appearances well into the fifth and final season, when Unger was reunited with his ex-wife.

Like her fellow cast members, Elinor was pleased to reunite for the two 1977 *Father Knows Best* specials. Old friendships were renewed and there was time to reminisce about the good times that more than outweighed the heavy work schedule.

In 1978, Elinor appeared in the made-for-TV film *Doctors' Private Lives*. She also starred in the comedy series *Please Stand By* as Carol, the bemused but patient wife of Frank, who abandons the corporate rat race to buy and operate a small-town television station. Viewers who remembered Donahue as Betty Anderson may have picked up on a little insider joke in one episode. Frank tells Carol that he has to cut some shows from the station's schedule. One of the shows he mentions is *Father Knows Best*. At which Carol says, "You wouldn't dare!"

Elinor's guest appearances were fewer in the 1980s, but included *Happy Days*, *Newhart*, and *The Golden Girls*. She also was featured in another TV film, *High School U.S.A.*

In 1990, Elinor was back on the big screen, this time playing a Beverly Hills clothing store manager who helps to upgrade prostitute Julia Roberts' wardrobe in *Pretty Woman*. From September 23, 1990, to March 8, 1992, she costarred with Chris Elliott and his real-life father Bob Elliott (of the Bob and Ray comedy duo) in the somewhat wacky comedy series *Get A Life*, about a 30-year-old paperboy living in an apartment above his parents' garage. She also branched out into voice acting as the mother of the Fox Kids on the 1992 animated series *Eek! The Cat*. She appeared as herself in Paramount Pictures' 1996 comedy *Dear God* (not to be confused with *Oh, God!* in which George Burns took on the title role).

Between 1993 and 1997, she made repeated appearances as Rebecca Quinn, sister of Dr. Michaela Quinn on the Western series *Dr. Quinn, Medicine Woman*.

Moving into the new century, Donahue appeared in the 2001 made-for-TV film *Dr. Quinn, Medicine Woman: The Heart Within*. In 2004, she won the TV Land Legend Award for her performance on *The Andy Griffith Show*. That year she also appeared in the film *The Princess Diaries 2: Royal Engagement*. As recently as 2010 and

2011, she has made incidental appearances on *The Young and the Restless*.

In 1962, Elinor married TV executive producer Harry Ackerman. She became stepmother to his daughter Susan and son Stephen. Together, they produced four sons, Brian, Peter, James and Chris. As of this writing, Elinor has seven grandchildren. Ackerman, who was some years older than Elinor, died in 1991. In 1992, she married Louis Genevrino, a former Broadway dancer, and they now are enjoying their senior years together at their home in the Coachella Valley.

When not performing, one of Donahue's favorite pastimes has long been getting creative in the kitchen. In 1998, she published her book *In the Kitchen with Elinor Donahue*. Along with memories of her acting career, she shares 150 of her favorite recipes.

Elinor Donahue, Billy Gray, and Lauren Chapin became close during their time together on *Father Knows Best*, and they have kept in touch over the years. Elinor and Billy are still in California, while Lauren makes her home in Florida. During a recent trip to the West Coast, Lauren visited with both Elinor and Billy.

———

REMEMBERING ROBERT YOUNG

If the Academy of Motion Picture Arts and Sciences had an Oscar for the category of Actor Most Frequently Called "Nice Guy," Robert Young would have been in the running every year while he worked for Metro-Goldwyn-Mayer. Even while struggling to hide the nagging depression that haunted him for years, he approached his profession with a work ethic that made him always a well-prepared and cooperative part of the team. He knew his lines, his marks, his cues, and was patient and helpful with fellow performers who came less well prepared.

Directors described Bob as the most unstarlike star. He worked hard, was dependable, sought direction, and apologized for occasional fluffs of his lines. His soft good looks, amiable personality, and the fact that he never attempted to steal a scene, made him a popular casting choice for many of the leading ladies at MGM who would play opposite him.

The Robert Young seen by all but a few of those closest to him was surely the most impressive performance of a long and versatile career. He was, as he described himself, an introvert in an extrovert profession. Interviewed when he was sixty-five, he said, "All those years at MGM, I hid a black terror behind a cheerful face. Every year I expected to be dropped"

What Robert didn't understand until years later was that he was not supposed to have any sense of security simply because he had a contract. In Hollywood's early years, before actors began to unionize, the industry was ruled by its motion picture tycoons and moguls. As smaller studios merged or were swallowed up by larger ones, five major studios came to dominate the film industry. Part of their standard operating procedure was to insure that actors were not permitted to feel serene, fulfilled, satisfied, or contented. The objective was to keep them insecure, and thus manageable.

In Robert's case, such studio tactics played handily upon his natural sense of insecurity. In the 1970s, having survived his years as a B picture film star and moved on to two successful television series, he and Betty gave a rare dual interview. Bob spoke of his ever-present fear of failing and recalled how he had hidden the pain that friends unknowingly inflicted upon him when they jokingly recalled Louis B. Mayer's comment about his lack of sex appeal. At that point, Bob's red-haired, mostly quiet wife interrupted to say, "I never complained about your sex appeal." Bob laughed and patted her hand. "No, you never did," he agreed, and he noted that they had four beautiful daughters to prove it.

As a footnote to that interview, Betty at one point commented, "Bobby and I always put our family first. I guess that's why he's able to be such a convincing father on the screen." Thus we learn that Betty apparently was the only person ever to call Robert "Bobby."

It seems likely that memories of what he, his mother, and his siblings had endured when his father deserted them influenced his strong sense of family closeness. No matter the ups and downs of his professional life, he found refuge and comfort in the family fold. Daughter Carol said he always looked forward to dinner at home and that Friday night movie with his ladies.

Robert jokingly acknowledged that he was out-numbered and often out-voted by his womenfolk, but he took it in stride. He recalled his *Father Knows Best* role being put to the test one day when one of his daughters asked him a question and he was obliged to reply, "I don't know." With a show of hands-on-hips indignation, she said, "But Jim Anderson always knows." His answer to that was, "Well, Jim Anderson has a lot of very smart writers, and I don't."

During his years with MGM, being pigeonholed as a B picture player, Robert continually wrestled with a conviction that he was a failure. Yet his family lived in a large home where the help included a cook, a maid, a twice-a-week laundress, a caretaker, and two nurses.

At one time, the Youngs owned a small farm in Carmel Valley. Why a farm? Bob, of course, was a city boy. So, if it was a working farm, he must have had hired help who knew how to run it. Perhaps a back-up in case his film career crashed? More likely, it was an idle farm where the family could enjoy weekend getaways.

Yet, in spite of his shy, introverted nature and constant fear of failing, Robert had a spirit of adventure in him. In addition to his sporty MG automobile, he once owned a motorcycle. Billy

Gray once saw him on it and later recalled that it was an Indian. Robert became part of an informal cycle club that included Clark Gable, Robert Montgomery, Ward Bond, director Victor Fleming, and several other male stars. In pairs, or in a group, they would at times get together for exhilarating rides on the open highway.

In 1947, he became interested in flying, took lessons, and soon acquired a pilot's license. He bought a small plane and flew to Carmel Valley at least once a month to check on things at the farm. Billy Gray recalled once being invited to join Bob on a round-trip flight to Santa Barbara.

When an interviewer asked Robert why he had left films for television, he said, "Films were already changing into what they are today when I became 'available' in 1962. The kind of role I was supposedly best suited for—light romantic comedy leads—no longer existed. Feature films, you might say, passed me by."

On another occasion, asked to name his favorite movie role, he unhesitatingly selected *The Enchanted Cottage*. "The role symbolized my own life," he explained, "though I wasn't a veteran who returned from war tragically disfigured. It demonstrated that we are all, somehow, handicapped. Shyness and fear of people were my invisible scars. These were finally overcome, just as in the movie, because of the love of a woman who saw the 'perfect man' through all the imperfections." He always felt that his long-sought recovery was made possible only with the aid and encouragement of his beloved Elizabeth.

Despite his personal problems, Robert was a very civic-minded man, finding it difficult to say "no." In addition to his leading role in a campaign to promote safe teen driving, he did promotions for the Boy Scouts of America, addressed a group of junior fire marshals, helped promote the March of Dimes, was a speaker for the American Federation of Women's Clubs, and was active in the local PTA. As the familiar television father, he received between 700 and 1000 requests annually to do everything from spearheading a Community Chest drive to addressing a high school graduating class. Of necessity, he had to pick and choose. Often it was a difficult choice because, as he explained, "I am inherently shy. I don't move easily in crowds."

He also did occasional public service films, but had to be extremely selective. People asking did not understand, he explained, that besides the cost of filming there was the loss of time. "It's ironic," he said. "When I was at MGM, I had plenty of time, but I didn't get one request."

Late in life, Robert was once asked about his depression and alcohol problems. "I was full of terror and fright," he confessed. "I drank to escape reality." After his unsuccessful suicide attempt in 1991, when he had gone public about his difficulty, he was chosen as Honorary Chairman of National Health Week. He spoke candidly about his personal problems in an effort to encourage others to seek help.

When he heard about Illinois Tax Referendum 708 back in his home state, Robert became an ardent supporter. The proposal was to establish a tax fund earmarked for the establishment of a center for patients with substance abuse and mental health problems. Robert gave his public endorsement to the proposal and was vocal in his support of the idea. He made a generous donation to the campaign for passage, and asked friends to do likewise.

The referendum passed. The first facility was built in Rock Island and was named The Robert Young Center for Community Mental Health. Two more facilities were later established in Moline and the Quad Cities area.

In spite of his pervading sense of insecurity and fear of failure, Robert George Young persevered in his chosen occupation, and he is deserving of multiple kudos.

He entertained millions of filmgoers in light comedies, dramas, romances, and even musicals.

He entertained millions of listeners on radio, and still more millions of viewers on two television series, all of which won accolades and awards.

He was the first to win Emmys as the star of both a comedy series and a drama.

His public service efforts ranked with those of Hollywood's most active stars.

He starred in two films that were nominated for Best Picture awards, *Crossfire* and *House of Rothschild*.

He was considered by many directors to be Hollywood's most unstrained star, and was a favorite co-star of many actresses.

Counting his made-for-television specials, his years with Metro-Goldwyn-Mayer, and as a freelancer, he appeared in over one hundred films, mostly in starring roles. That's an impressive record, even if most of the films were B pictures.

By all accounts, Robert George Young was one of those people that you just couldn't help but like.

Perhaps most commendable of all, in spite of his fears and frustrations, he was a devoted husband and father for whom family always came first.

———

At Jane Wyatt's request, Billy Gray was one of Robert's pallbearers. At the funeral, she was seen leaning on Billy's shoulder.

Remembering their years together on the *Father Knows Best* series, Wyatt recalled his fatherly encouragement of the three young cast members. "What Bob taught those three children about acting could fill a book," she said. "His secret was in treating the kids as adult actors rather than children. He was a perfectionist, and he insisted on perfection from everyone." On her own feeling toward Young, Wyatt said, "Bob was a wonderful actor to work with and one of the most conscientious people I have ever known. He couldn't have been more generous in the sense of sharing, not only the good material with the other actors, but also sharing the credit for the show's success."

Robert and Elizabeth's daughter Carol put it simply: "Daddy was a very thoughtful, caring person." Her sister Betty added, "The world has lost one of its last real leading men, and I have lost my father."

Robert was honored with three stars on Hollywood's Walk of Fame: one for film (6933 Hollywood Blvd.), one for television (6358 Hollywood Blvd.), and one for radio (1660 Vine St.).

Robert George Young dealt with multiple troubles and fears that he kept hidden from most of the world. But with perseverance and the unfailing support of his beloved Elizabeth, he endured. Still quiet and humble at the final curtain, he nonetheless could answer the curtain call, take a well-earned bow, and exit triumphant.

ACKNOWLEDGEMENTS

Writing a book can be a lonesome endeavor, but I was fortunate to have a lot of company along the way, albeit sporadic. I cannot conclude without a word of gratitude.

When he is not earning his living as a professional architect, Bob Kolososki can usually be found pursuing his avocation of film historian, with a focus on the black and white films of the 1950s and going back to the silent pictures era. In addition to providing a fine foreword, Bob was my fact checker for all the film references herein. With his knowledge of films and the people who starred in them, he checked me for inaccuracies and provided some Hollywood background information, including some tidbits about our subject, Robert Young

Stephen Cox has written more books than I typically read in a year. His *One Fine Stooge* is a "must have" for fans of the Three Stooges. Steve also has an impressive photo collection of things Hollywood, the films and their stars. He provided several of the latter, and all of those swell film stills are from his collection.

I wanted to include a photo of all the young folk who filled various roles in the radio and television versions of *Father Knows Best*. It was at first a frustrating search. Then Drina Mohacsi, proprietor of the *Young Hollywood* website, came to my rescue. The site, which can be found at *www.YoungHollywoodHOF.com*, is a collection of photos, by decade, of all the young actors and actresses, many of them long forgotten, who graced the screen going back to the silent film era. Drina rounded up photos of almost all the juvenile performers on my list.

Steve Darnall, editor-publisher of the quarterly *Nostalgia Digest*, provided a promo photo of the *Father Knows Best* television cast and one of Robert Young at the NBC microphone, as well as a couple of anecdotes about Robert.

When I contacted the Abraham Lincoln High School in Los Angeles, Librarian Lily Moayeri and Alumni Association representative Robert Granados teamed up to track down period photos of the school and a collection of yearbook photos, including Elizabeth Henderson, Robert Young, scenes of Playcrafters performances and more.

Ross Clark, a volunteer archivist at the Pasadena Playhouse sent me photos of the Playhouse, one of its theaters, and some on-stage scenes in which Robert appears. He also included a complete list of every performance in which Robert took part during his years at the School of Theatre Arts, including what roles he played.

Tricia Gesner at the Associated Press guided me through the maze of their photo archive and found almost two dozen photos of Robert and his family, including my favorite, that swell picture of Robert in his airplane.

Technically, I am supposed to tell you that the photo of Dorothy Lovett is courtesy of the Margaret Herrick Library and the Academy of Motion Picture Arts and Sciences. But when none of my usual sources were able to come up with a photo, librarian Genevieve Maxwell and her assistant Bijan were the heroes who came to my rescue. They found a batch of studio photos in an Academy museum collection, and it included that perfect one of Lovett posed before a radio microphone.

Lauren Chapin, Elinor Donahue, and Billy Gray all were kind enough to answer many questions and share some recollections from their years in the *Father Knows Best* television cast. They all provided some photos from their personal collections. Billy produced one of my favorites, Robert Young on his motorcycle. Lauren's photo of Robert skipping rope with her is a treasure.

Elinor does not do computers, so we were not able to communicate via email. Instead, we relied upon the old faithful U. S. Postal Service. Elinor gave detailed responses to my questions and added many personal notes in more than two dozen pages of handwritten responses! She gets an A+ for Effort.

Laurie McGuire applied her editorial skills first to proofreading the text, then making suggestions to fine-tune, reword, or reorganize here and there.

Tech-savvy Jennifer McGuire guided me through processing and organizing photos, and kept me functioning when my minimal computer skills bogged down.

By taking on the chore of all outdoor maintenance at our home, David McGuire freed me to do research and try to turn it into a page or two of copy per day.

Finally, I would not have gotten through this project were it not for the patience of my dear wife Joy, who kept our household functioning while I disappeared for hours into the computer den, and only interrupted to see that I ate three meals a day. She did, occasionally, call on me to take the garbage out.

To all whose assistance and encouragement helped get me to the completion of this book, my most grateful thanks.

Dan McGuire

ABOUT THE AUTHOR

Dan McGuire is an octogenarian who has been a long-time contributor to the quarterly magazine *Nostalgia Digest*. His first book, *Now, When I Was A Kid*, is a collection of articles from the magazine that recall fun times growing up back in the days when moms called their kids home from the front porch rather than on their cell phones.

He subsequently had two books published by BearManor Media. *Old-Time Radio's Comedy Couples* covers the lives and careers of five couples (can you name them?) who were married both on their programs and in real life. *The Two Great Gildersleeves* recalls one program and the two actors who filled the lead role, Harold Peary and Willard Waterman.

Dan and his wife Joy still abide in the home where they reared elder daughter Laurie and twins David and Jennifer. While self-isolated during the Covid-19 pandemic, they celebrated their 60th wedding anniversary there with a quiet candlelight dinner.